# The Parables of Jesus

*Student Workbook*

*A Small Group Bible Study*

*Part One*

*Linda Marie Quiggle*

# Copyright

# Acknowledgments

Scripture quotations marked CJB are taken from the Complete Jewish Bible. Copyright © 1998 by David H. Stern.

Scripture quotations marked DARBY are taken from the Darby Bible. This Bible is in the public domain in the United States.

Scripture quotations marked ERV are taken from the Easy-to-Read Version. Copyright © 2006 by Bible League International.

Scripture quotations marked ESV are taken from The Holy Bible, English Standard Version. Copyright © 2000, 2001 by Crossway Bibles, A Division of Good News Publishers, 1300 Crescent Street, Wheaton, Illinois 60187, USA. All rights reserved.

Scripture quotations marked HCSB are taken from the Holman Christian Standard Bible, Copyright 1999, 2000, 2002, 2003, by Holman Bible Publishers. Scripture quotations marked HCSB are from the Holman Christian Standard Bible®, Copyright © 1999, 2000, 2002, 2003 by Holman Bible Publishers. Used by permission. Holman Christian Standard Bible®, Holman CSB®, and HCSB® are federally registered trademarks of Holman Bible Publishers.

Scripture quotations marked JDQT are taken from the Translations of Select Bible books by James D. Quiggle. Copyright @ 2018, Create Space.

Scripture quotations marked KJV are taken from the King James Version. The King James Version present on the Bible Gateway matches the 1987 printing. The KJV is public domain in the United States.

Scripture quotations marked MSG are taken from The Message. Copyright © 1993, 1994, 1995, 1996, 2000, 2001, 2002. Used by permission of NavPress Publishing Group.

Scripture quotations marked NASB are taken from the New American Standard Bible Translation. © The Lockman Foundation. 1960, 1962, 1963, 1968, 1972, 1973, 1974, 1975, 1977. A Corporation Not For Profit. La Habra, CA. Used by permission. All Rights Reserved.

Scripture quotations marked NLT are taken from the Holy Bible, New Living Translation, copyright © 1996, 2004, 2015 by Tyndale House Foundation. Used by permission of Tyndale House Publishers, Inc., Carol Stream, Illinois 60188. All rights reserved.

Scripture quotations marked WYC are taken from the Wycliffe Bible. Copyright © 2001 by Terence P. Noble.

# Dedication

To my friend Janet Conley, thank you for letting the Holy Spirit lead you to choose the parables as a topic for the Haven Bible Class. It was a joyous event leading our class through them and the inspiration for this book.

To my friend Eunabeth Williamson, thank you for always being willing to help me find "just the right song" and sharing your Israel trip pictures for my book covers.

To my late friend and pastor, David Hollingsworth, and my friends and young adult leaders Dick and Shirly Carpenter, thank you for mentoring me as a young woman and setting my feet firmly on the heavenly road.

To my life–long friend and faithful copy editor, Kathy Hollingsworth. Without your input this book would be so much less.

To James Quiggle, my husband and very best friend, thank you for teaching me how to think outside of the box and ask myself questions when rightly dividing the word of truth.

# Table of Contents

**The Purpose of Parables**.................................................................................i

**The Interpretation of Parables**................................................................ iii

**To the Students** .........................................................................................V

Chapter One: **The Salt of the Earth** ......................................................1
Matthew 5:13; Luke 14:34–35

Chapter Two: **The Light of the World** ...................................................5
Matthew 5:14–15; Mark 4:21–23; Luke 8:16–18; Luke 11:33–36

Chapter Three: **Blasphemy Against the Holy Spirit** ............................9
Matthew 12:22–32; Mark 3:22–30; Luke 5:36–38

Chapter Four: **Good Tree or Bad Tree?** ...............................................17
Matthew 12:33–37

Chapter Five: **On the Rock or On the Sand?** .......................................25
Matthew 7:24–27; Luke 6:46–49

Chapter Six: **The Old and the New** ......................................................29
Matthew 9:16–17; Mark 2:21–22; Luke 5:36–38

Chapter Seven: **A Woman and a Money Lender** .................................35
Luke 7:36–48

Chapter Eight: **Four Types of Soil** .......................................................41
Matthew 13:3–9; Matthew 13:18–23

Chapter Nine: **The Seed Growing Secretly**.........................................47
Mark 4:26–29

Chapter Ten: **The Sower, the Wheat, and the Weeds**.........................51
Matthew 13:24–29; Matthew 13:36–43

Chapter Eleven: **The Mustard Seed** ....................................................55
Matthew 13:31–32; Mark 4:30–32; Luke 13:18–19

Chapter Twelve: **The Leaven** ...............................................................59
Matthew 13:33; Luke 13:20

Chapter Thirteen: **3 Short Parables About the Kingdom of Heaven** ......................63
Matthew 13:44–50

Chapter Fourteen: **The Lost Sheep and the Lost Coin** ............................69
Matthew 18:12–14; Luke 15:3–10

Chapter Fifteen: **The Unforgiving Slave** ....................................79
Matthew 18:23–34

Chapter Sixteen: **The Sheep, The Door and The Good Shepherd** ...........85
John 10:1–30

Chapter Seventeen: **The Samaritan Who Was a Friend** .................. 103
Luke 10:25–37

Chapter Eighteen: **A Friend in Need and How to Pray** .................. 111
Luke 11:1–13

Chapter Nineteen: **Foolishly Preoccupied** ........................... 117
Luke 12:13–23

*The Author's Closing Remarks* ........................ 123

Appendix One: **Fig Trees** .......................... 127

Appendix Two: **Dispensationalism** ........................ 129

Appendix Three: **John Calvin** .......................... 135

Appendix Four: **The Jewish and Modern Calendar, Jewish Festivals,**

   **and Jewish Harvests** .......................... 137

Appendix Five: **Timeline of the Ages** ........................ 143

Appendix Six: **Exorcism and Exorcists** ........................ 145

Appendix Seven: **Tyrian Purple Dye** ........................ 149

Appendix Eight: **Linen and Flax** ........................ 151

Appendix Nine: **Skin Diseases: Boils** ........................ 155

Appendix Ten: **Ancient Jewish Courts and Judicial System** ........................ 157

Appendix Eleven: **Widows** ........................ 161

Appendix Twelve: **Pharisees** ........................................................ 163

Appendix Thirteen: **Ancient Jewish Tax Collectors and System** ........................... 165

Appendix Fourteen: **Beg, Beggar, Begging** ..................................... 169

Appendix Fifteen: **The Unpardonable Sin** ................................. 173

Appendix Sixteen: **Venomous Snakes** ................................. 177

Appendix Seventeen: **The Rapture and Tribulation** ......................... 179

Appendix Eighteen: **Four Kingdoms in Scripture**................................181

References................................................................. 185

# The Purpose for Parables

## Mark 4:10–12 (MSG)

*"10–12  When they were off by themselves, those who were close to him, along with the Twelve, asked about the stories. He told them, "You've been given insight into God's kingdom—you know how it works. But to those who can't see it yet, everything comes in stories, creating readiness, nudging them toward receptive insight. These are people—*

*Whose eyes are open but don't see a thing, whose ears are open but don't understand a word, who avoid making an about–face and getting forgiven."*

The words spoken by Jesus in Mark 4:10–12 are very similar to the words God spoke to Isaiah in Isaiah 6:9–10.

> "God told the prophet to deliver his message even though it would be rejected.  The seeing without perceiving, the hearing without understanding, and the failure to turn and be forgive (Isaiah wrote "be healed") were the <u>result</u>, not the purpose of his message.
>
> "So it was also with the parables of Jesus… Jesus did not speak in parables for the purpose of withholding truth from anyone; but the result of his parables, the rest of his teaching, and even his miracles was that most did not understand and respond positively.
>
> "He did speak  in parables to provoke thought and invite commitment.  Therefore parables are more than mere illustrations.  They constitute spiritual tests that separate those who understand and believe from  those who do not."
>
> *(Brooks 1991)*

# The Interpretation of Parables

**NOTE:** I approach all my Bible study with a "dispensational" view. (For an explanation of dispensationalism please read Appendix Two.)

Allegorizing, or symbolizing, has been a deadly poison to parable interpretation over the centuries. Turning the tide on this interpretation style, by emphasizing that parables have a single, main point to make was largely the work of theologian A. Jülicher, followed by the influential books of C.H. Dodd and J. Jeremias.

Dodd and Jeremias more completely recognized that this point needed to be discovered by seeing it through the historical setting of the ministry of Jesus and the early Church. This type of exegesis served as a commonsense answer against the insipid teaching of the parables in the fashion of Aesop's fables that totally overlooked the drama of the end times as regarded the parables. Dodd and Jeremias interpreted the meaning of the parables by insisting that they be interpreted by the life settings, the culture, of Jesus in the first century instead of by the life settings of theirs and our current cultures.

That single point, determined by a grammatical–historical exegesis of the parables, has gradually given way to the idea that the parables have a *multivalence of meanings* (the quality or state of having many values, meanings, or appeals) and the free creation of their meaning can be based on the personal situation of the reader.

Now, there are allegorical elements in many of the parables, not just those interpreted allegorically by Jesus. Concern over the abuse of allegorizing the parables should not stop the interpreter, the teacher, from giving mindful consideration to these elements. At the same time, you should not simply accept all allegorizing at face value. Only those allegorical elements that are relatively clear based on the context of the Gospel itself and that may be accurately recognized without compromising the single main point of the parable or its historical meaning, should be acceptable.

Every reader brings their own baggage and ideas that are bound to affect the interpretation of a text. Just because we recognize this paradigm, does not mean that we have to submit to the conclusion that the text has no meaning in and of itself, or that the meaning of a text (and its author) is outside of the reader's ability to grasp.

The involvement of the reader in the interpretation of the parables is to be desired since they, the parables, are a language event (a theory that Jesus' words and deeds constituted that "language event" in which faith first entered into language.) and are also informative. That is, they are intended to have an impact on the reader at whatever spiritual level of maturity the reader might find themselves. The parables don't exist simply to convey information.

It is still necessary to understand a parable in the historical contexts of the first century, but without reducing the parable only to historical information. As the parables grabbed their initial hearers and readers, so they need to grab the contemporary reader; experiencing the power, understanding with their heart as well as their head, and responding not only to the historical information, but more importantly, to the personal call of God on their lives through the Parables of Jesus.

# To the Students

The intent of this study is that there will be NO HOMEWORK for participants but that each question and scripture verse will be read aloud, discussed, and completed in class as a group.

 THIS BOOK SYMBOL INDICATES YOU NEED TO LOOK UP SOMETHING AND READ IT ALOUD IN CLASS

THIS PENCIL SYMBOL INDICATES YOU NEED TO DO SOME WRITING IN CLASS

THE SPEAKING HEAD MEANS YOU NEED TO ENGAGE IN SOME DISCUSSION IN CLASS

THIS COFFEE CUP SYMBOL INVITES YOU TO TAKE A MOMENT & THINK ABOUT WHAT IS SAID

THE HAND TO THE EAR INDICATES, PAY ATTENTION TO WHAT THE TEACHER IS ABOUT TO EXPLAIN

# Chapter One

## *The Salt of the Earth*
Matthew 5:13; Luke 14:34–35

**📖 Matthew 5:13; 📖 Luke 14:34–35**

**Who are the characters or items in this parable?**

_____

**When is the story told?**

_____

**Where is the story told?**

_____

**Who is in the audience?**

_____

Matthew 5:13 "...You..."

**Who is the "You"?**

_____

📖 Colossians 4:6

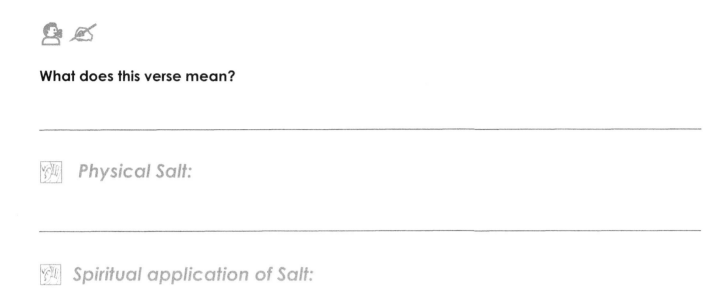

**What does this verse mean?**

_____

*Physical Salt:*

_____

*Spiritual application of Salt:*

_____

*We are commanded to be useful salt, not useless dregs..*

*Figure 1 – The Dead Sea in Israel being*

*harvested for salt*

A salt evaporation pond is a shallow artificial salt pan designed to extract salts from sea water or other brines....The seawater or brine is fed into large ponds and water is drawn out through natural evaporation which allows the salt to be subsequently harvested.

www.wikipedia.com

# Chapter Two

## *The Light of the World*
Matthew 5:14–15; Mark 4:21–23; Luke 8:16–18; Luke 11:33–36

📖 **Matthew 5:14–15**   📖 **Mark 4:21–23 (HCSB)**
📖 **Luke 8:16–18 (NASB)**   📖 **Luke 11:33–36 (NASB)**

**Who are the characters or items in this parable?**

_____

**When is the story told?**

_____

**Where is the story told?**

_____

**Who is in the audience?**

_____

Beds in Bible times were nothing like the beds we know today in the 21st century. Most people slept on a mat spread on the floor. During the day, the mats were rolled up and stored. Sometimes the mats were placed on a raised platform, above cold drafts during the wintertime. When this was done, "things" would be stored under it, similar to what can be found under our beds centuries later.

## Hear Correctly

# I Have Seen the Light

I was a seeker for light in a dark world,
I looked for truth but settled for lies.
I had been blinded; I couldn't see
Till the Star in Bethlehem's sky opened my eyes.
I have seen the Light shining in the darkness,
Bursting through the shadows, delivering the dawn.
I have seen the Light whose holy name is Jesus,
His kingdom is forever; He reigns on Heaven's throne!
There in a manger, an innocent baby;
Who could believe He was the One;
I can believe it, I know it's true;
He changed my life; He is the light; He is God's Son!
I have seen the Light shining in the darkness,
Bursting through the shadows, delivering the dawn.
I have seen the Light whose holy name is Jesus,
His kingdom is forever; He reigns on Heaven's throne!
We must tell the world what we`ve seen today in Bethlehem!
He`s the promised King; we bow down and worship Him!
Worship Christ The King!
I have seen the Light shining in the darkness,
Bursting through the shadows, delivering the dawn.
I have seen the Light whose holy name is Jesus,
His kingdom is forever; He reigns on Heaven's throne!

Blake Bolerjack/Christmas Light album, November 18, 2011

# Chapter Three

## *Blasphemy Against the Holy Spirit*
Matthew 12:22–32;  Mark 3:22–30; Luke 12:10–12

📖 **Matthew 12:22–32**   📖 **Mark 3:22–30**   📖 **Luke 12:10–12**

**Who are the characters or items in this parable?**

_____

**When is the story told?**

_____

**Where is the story told?**

_____

**Who is in the audience?**

_____

_____

_____

_____

_____

🍵  FYI – Everyone who is blind and cannot speak are NOT autmatically  possessed by an evil spirit.

## The Crowd Was Amazed

---

*It wasn't that they were challenging the obvious fact that Jesus had power, it was the "source" of that power that seemed to stump them.*

---

## The Preposterous Explanation

📖 **Matthew 12:24**

---

> "That is the last resort, of prejudice so deep, that it will father an absurdity rather than yield to evidence…. There is an old play which has for its title, '*The Devil as an Ass*.' He is not such an ass as that, to build up with one hand and cast down with the other. As the proverb has it, 'Hawks do not pick out hawks' eyes.'"
>
> *(Maclaren Reprinted 1977)*

## The Parable

  📖 **Matthew 12:25**   📖 **Mark 3:23–27**

## He knew their hearts

_____

_____

_____

_____

## How can Satan, cast out Satan?

  📖 **Matthew 12:24–25**  📖 **Mark 3:26**

_____

_____

_____

_____

## Jesus Confronts the Pharisees

  📖 **Matthew 12:27–28**

For background information on "Exorcism and Exorcists" in the time of Jesus, see Appendix Six.

## A Strong Man and Someone Stronger

📖 **Matthew 12:29** 📖 **Mark 3:27**

## With Me or Against Me?

📖 **Matthew 12:30**

Jesus now changes his tone. Up to now he has reasoned with the Pharisees, but now He severely admonishes them.

## The Statement Concerning Blasphemy

### 📖 **Matthew 12:31–32**   📖 **Mark 3:28–30**   📖 **Luke 12:10–12**

Let's establish a definition for the word "Blasphemy" before we apply it to the Holy Spirit.

📖 👤 ✒

**How does an online dictionary define blasphemy?**

_____

_____

**How does Strong's Concordance define blasphemy?**

_____

_____

**How does a Bible Dictionary define blasphemy?**

_____

_____

For an in-depth discussion on the "Unpardonable Sin" and whether it can be committed today, see Appendix Fifteen.

# Speaking Against the Son of Man versus the Holy Spirit

📖 **Matthew 12:32**

> "The difference is the deity of the Son of Man is a truth that must be revealed to the person by the Holy Spirit.
>
> "Therefore speaking against Jesus Christ is not unforgivable, because the unsaved person lacks the knowledge, understanding, and conviction given by the Holy Spirit to know that Jesus Christ is the God–Man.
>
> "The Holy Spirit is the Person who reveals the truth to the sinner, convicts the sinner of sin, the Savior, and salvation, and applies Christ's saving merit to save the sinner. The Holy Spirit is the means whereby the gift of God—which is grace–faith–salvation (Ephesians 2:8)—is applied to the unsaved person. The work of the Holy Spirit is the bridge (an analogy) between election and salvation:
>
> ### 2 Thessalonians 2:13 (HCSB)
>
> > 13 'But we must always thank God for you, brothers loved by the Lord, because from the beginning God has chosen you for salvation [election] through sanctification by the Spirit [regeneration] and through belief in the truth [faith].'
>
> ### 1 Peter 1:2 (ESV)
>
> > 2 'Who have been chosen [election] according to the foreknowledge of God the Father, in the sanctification of the Spirit [regeneration], for obedience to Jesus Christ [faith] and for sprinkling with his blood [salvation]: May grace and peace be multiplied to you.'
>
> "If the Holy Spirit is an unclean spirit, then he is unable to effect the salvation relationship with God through Christ. Does blasphemy against the Spirit prevent him from working? Yes, because God has given a law and its punishment. The law is, 'Whoever should blaspheme the Holy Spirit is guilty of an eternal sin.' The punishment for violating that law is, 'No forgiveness forever.'
>
> "We should not be surprised that there is a sin for which there is no forgiveness. We have an example in the fallen angels, who never have forgiveness forever, but are guilty of an eternal sin. So, too it is, with the blasphemy of the Holy Spirit."
>
> *(J. D. Quiggle, Hermeneutics: Blasphemy Against the Holy Spirit 2019)*

# Chapter Four

## *Good Tree or Bad Tree?*
Matthew 12:33–37

## 📖 Matthew 12:33–37

🗣️ ✍️

**Who are the characters or items in this parable?**

_____

**When is the story told?**

_____

**Where is the story told?**

_____

**Who is in the audience?**

_____

👂 🗣️ ✍️

This short parable follows directly after Jesus speaks these words:

### Matthew 12:32 (ESV)

> *32 Anyone who speaks against the Son of Man can be forgiven, but anyone who speaks against the Holy Spirit will never be forgiven, either in this world or in the world to come.*

_____

_____

_____

_____

📖 **Matthew 12:33a**

And if a tree does not bear an edible fruit (apple, pear, date), it still has characteristics that can make it a good tree or a bad tree. Don't some of those tree descriptions remind you of yourself or others?

# Characteristics of Trees

"Hackberry" - Although *Celtis occidentalis* is an important tree in regions where alkaline soils are problematic, it is a poor substitute when other species are options. The tree has weak wood and messy in the landscape. It grows very large and hard to manage in the landscape.

"Norway Maple" - *Acer platanoides* was introduced into North Ameria over 200 years ago and has aggressively spread taking over native maple populations. The invasive nature of the tree degrades most landscapes over time.

"Silver Maple" - *Acer saccharinum* is a maple with some of the weakest wood of the native North American maple. It has a very short natural life and suffers continually from breakage and disease.

"Mimosa" - *Albizia julibrissin* or silk tree is a warm-climate invasive exotic and was widely planted for its beautiful flower and beauty in the landscape. It is subject to a major wilt disease and very messy in the landscape.

"Lombardy poplar" - *Populus nigra* is a North American exotic with absolutely no redeeming features according to most horticulturists. It has been planted mainly as a windbreak but is short-lived and quickly loses even that ability.

"Leyland cypress" - *Cupressocyparis leylandii* has been widely planted as hedges over the last three decades. It is now out of favor to plant in all but the most expansive landscapes. Planting them too close and a major disease makes them undesirable in the urban landscape.

"Pin Oak" - Quercus palustris is actually a very beautiful tree under optimal conditions. Like Leyland cypress, the oak needs a large area in maturity and is subject sensitive to many soil conditions common to many yards and landscapes.

"Cottonwood" - *Populus deltoides* is another weak-wooded tree, messy, massive and has an overwhelming spring shedding of reproductive parts. It still is a favorite where trees are scarce.

"Willow" - *Salix* spp. is a beautiful "weeping" tree in the right landscape, especially in wetlands and near aquatic ecosystems. For these same reasons, it does not make a desirable yard tree because of the need for space and for its destructive tendency to destroy water pipes.

"Black Locust" - *Robinia pseudoacacia* has a place on our native forests, and even there can become invasive. This "tree of thorns" really has no place in a landscape enjoyed by visitors. It is also a heavy sprouter/seeder and can quickly overtake even large landscapes.

https://www.thoughtco.com/yard-trees-gone-bad-1343518

I have Hackberry trees in and around my house. They are messy. They are intrusive. In the spring and fall, they make my allergies go crazy. I would never want to be compared to one. And yet, they provide such excellent shade for my house, and the birds and squirrels make their homes in them. My dog loves to eat the berries that grow on them. Is it a good tree or a bad tree? Yes. Just like the "born again" person that has the "old nature battling against the new nature" (📖 Romans 7:14–15), the Hackberry tree has good and bad characteristics.

## 📖 Matthew 12:33b

_____

_____

_____

## Brood of Snakes

## 📖 Matthew 12:34

_____

_____

_____

Read Appendix Sixteen to gain a greater appreciation for what vipers are and how many of the characteristics of the Pharisees are similar to those of vipers.

## 📖 Matthew 12:35

_____

_____

## I Tell You This

## 📖 Matthew 12:36

_____

_____

_____

## Acquit or Condemn

## 📖 Matthew 12:37

Let's establish a definition for the words Acquit and Condemn.

**How does an online dictionary define <u>Acquit</u>?**

_____

**How does an online dictionary define <u>Condemn</u>?**

_____

**How does Strong's Concordance define these two words?**

_____

_____

📖 👤 ✍

_____

_____

_____

# Questions to Ask Yourself:

1. Am I a good tree or a bad tree?

2. Do my words show I am saved or unsaved?

3. Do my words show I am still a baby in Christ, only able to drink milk, and not eat solid food?

4. Do my words show you have matured and become more like Christ?

5. Will I hear, "Well done, good and faithful servant?"

---

### Matthew 25:23 (ESV)

"His master said to him, 'Well done, good and faithful servant. You have been faithful over a little; I will set you over much.
Enter into the joy of your master.'"

---

# Chapter Five

## *On the Rock or On the Sand?*
Matthew 7:24–27; Luke 6:46–49

📖 **Matthew 7:24–27** 📖 **Luke 6:46–49**

**Who are the characters or items in this parable?**

_____

**When is the story told?**

_____

**Where is the story told?**

_____

**Who is in the audience?**

_____

_____

_____

_____

_____

_____

---

*Jesus' sermon was not concerned with the blueprints, material lists, construction practices or even building codes. His intention was a spiritual focus.*

---

In this world the wise person has faith and hope, and in the next everlasting life and love:

---

**1 Corinthians 13:13 (NLT)**

Three things will last forever—faith, hope, and love—and the greatest of these is love.

---

The wise man is also like a tree planted by the riverside:

---

**Psalm 1:1–3 (AMP)***

1 Blessed, [fortunate, prosperous, and favored by God] is the man who does not walk in the counsel of the wicked [following their advice and example], Nor stand in the path of sinners, Nor sit [down to rest] in the seat of scoffers (ridiculers).

2But his {the wise man's} delight is in the law of the Lord, and on His law {God's precepts and teachings} he {the wise man} [habitually] meditates day and night.

3 And he {the wise man} will be like a tree firmly planted [and fed] by streams of water,

Which yields its fruit in its season; Its leaf does not wither; and in whatever he {the wise man} does, he {the wise man} prospers [and comes to maturity].

*NOTE: * Items in [ ] are amplified explanations that are part of the Bible translation.  {} are clarifications by the author.*

---

# Chapter Six

## *The Old and the New*
Matthew 9:16–17; Mark 2:21–22; Luke 5:36–38

## 📖 **Matthew 9:16–17**  📖 **Mark 2:20–22**  📖 **Luke 5:36–38**

This parable is answering the question found in Matthew 9:14–15, Mark 2:18–22, Luke 5:33–34 concerning fasting.

**Who are the characters or items in this parable?**

_____

**When is the story told?**

_____

**Where is the story told?**

_____

**Who is in the audience?**

_____

_____

_____

_____

_____

## Fasting

Let's establish a definition for the word Fasting.

**How does an online dictionary define Fasting?**

_____

**How does Strong's Concordance define this word?**

_____

_____

*Examples of those who fasted:*

    **Exodus 34:28 – Who?** _____

    **1 Samuel 7:6 – Who?** _____

    **Jonah 3:5 – Who?** _____

    **1 Samuel 31:11–13 –Who?** _____

    **Daniel 6:15–21 – Who?** _____

Use a Concordance to find additional examples of fasting.

> **Semi–Weekly Fasts:** "It is said that these semi–weekly fasts were observed by the Jews because continuous fasting might be injurious. The days selected were the second and firth. The reason assigned for the selection of these days is because it was supposed to be on the second day of the week that Moses went up into Mount Sinai to receive the two tables of the law, and it was on the fifth day of the week that he came down on account of the idolatry concerning the golden calf. These days were chosen, not only when public fasts were to be observed, but also when individuals fasted privately.
>
> "The only fast commanded in the Mosaic law was in connection with the celebration of the Great Day of Atonement. (Leviticus 16:34) Other fasts were observed, however, in later periods of Jewish history until, in our Lord's time, the Pharisees carried the practice to an extreme. They fasted often, (Matthew 9:14) and disfigured their faces (Matthew 6:16). In the text the Pharisee is represented as regarding this frequent fasting as an evidence of his piety."
>
> *(J. D. Quiggle, A Private Commentary on the Bible: Matthew's Gospel 2017)*

## The Old Fabric with a New Patch

📖 **Luke 5:36**

_____

_____

_____

_____

## The Old Wineskin with New Wine

📖 **Luke 5:37–38**

**What were wineskins?** _____

**What were they made of?** _____

**How were they used?** _____

**Why wasn't new wine put into previously used wineskins?** _____

_____

**What is the point of this parable?**

_____

_____

_____

_____

*"The questions posed by the image of the wedding feast and the two atom–like parables is not whether disciples will, like sewing a new patch on an old garment or refilling an old container, make room for Jesus in their already full agendas and lives.  The question is whether they will forsake business as usual and join the wedding celebration; whether they will become entirely new receptacles for the expanding fermentation of Jesus and the gospel in their lives."[1]*

---
[1] (Edwards 2002)

# *Questions to Ask Yourself:*

- Am I willing to continue living the same old way?

- Am I eager to pursue an extraordinary life in Jesus?

- Am I willing to become an entirely new receptacle for the "fermentation of Jesus" in my life?

---

**Joshua 24:15 (DARBY)**

And if it seems evil unto you to serve Jehovah, choose you this day whom ye will serve...,
but as for me and my house, we will serve Jehovah.

---

# Chapter Seven

## *A Woman and a Money Lender*
Luke 7:36–48

### Prelude to the Parable
&#x1F4D6; **Luke 7:36–40**

### Parable
&#x1F4D6; **Luke 7:41–43**

### Application
&#x1F4D6; **Luke 7:44–50**

**Who are the characters or items in this parable?**

_____

**When is the story told?**

_____

**Where is the story told?**

_____

**Who is in the audience?**

_____

## The Meal

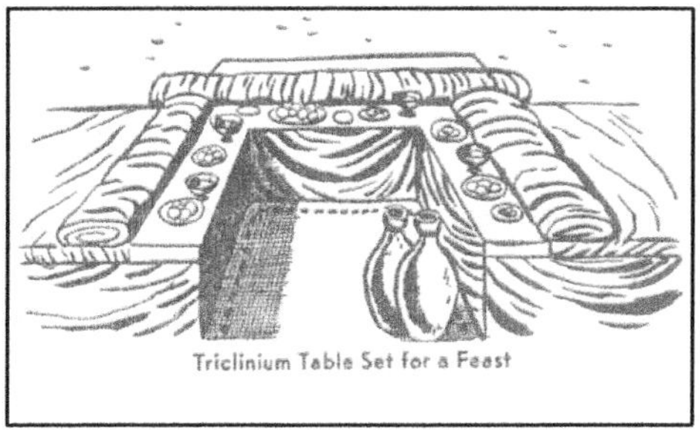

Figure 2: Fred H. Wight – Manners and Customs of Bible Lands

## The Dinner

"Unguent" means an ointment or salve, usually in a liquid or semiliquid state.

## Simeon and Jesus' Conversation

## The Parable

📖 **Luke 7:41–43**

_____

_____

_____

## The Application

📖 **Luke 7:44–46**

_____

_____

_____

_____

> *"Do you see this woman?  Did he? It is an interesting point. 'Simon could not see that woman as she <u>then was</u>, for looking at her as she <u>had been</u>.'"*[1]

[1] (Morris, Luke, an Introduction and Commentary (Tyndale New Testament Commentaries) Reprinted 1999)

## Cultural Norms

## *Broken and Spilled Out*

One day a plain village woman driven by love for her Lord
Recklessly poured out a valuable essence disregarding the scorn
And once it was broken and spilled out a fragrance filled all the room
Like a pris'ner released from his shackles like a spirit set free from the tomb

Broken and spilled out just for love of you Jesus
My most precious treasure lavished on Thee
Broken and spilled out and poured at Your feet
In sweet abandon let me be spilled out
And used up for Thee

Lord You were God's precious treasure His loved and His own perfect Son
Sent here to show me the love of the Father
Just for love it was done and though You were perfect and holy

You gave up Yourself willingly you spared no expense for my pardon
You were used up and wasted for me

Broken and spilled out just for love of me Jesus
God's most precious treasure lavished on me
You were broken and spilled out and poured at my feet
In sweet abandon Lord you were spilled out and used up for Me

In sweet abandon, let me be spilled out and used up for Thee

By Bill George and Gloria Gaithier

# Chapter Eight

## *Four Types of Soil*
Matthew 13:3–9; Matthew 13:18–23

##  Matthew 13:3–9 and 18–23

 This parable is also found in: <u>Mark</u> 4:2–9 and 14–20; <u>Luke</u> 8:4–8 and 11–15. Please read these accounts as well as the Matthew account printed above. Why? Just like a family that goes on a vacation together, taking pictures of this and that and each other, each individual comes back from that vacation with a slightly different point of view and different pictures. While *some sights* are seen by <u>all</u> of them, *not every sight* and *experience* (every meal, and every sunset) are experienced by <u>all</u> of them. It is also like that with the writings of Matthew, Mark, Luke, and John.

**Who are the characters or items in this parable?**

_____

**When is the story told?**

_____

**Where is the story told?**

_____

**Who is in the audience?**

_____

 Chapter twelve of Matthew ends in the house where Jesus lived when he visited Capernaum. After he had confronted the scribes and Pharisees, Jesus left the house to teach on the shore of the lake. Sitting was the position Jewish teachers assumed when teaching. By sitting in the boat he would force the crowds to spread out along the shoreline, limiting the depth of the crowd, and allowing everyone to be close enough to hear.

## Listen!

**Why does he start off with "Listen!"?**

## The Parable

### 📖 **Matthew 13:3b–8**

### 📖 **Matthew 13:9**

First He says, "Listen!" and now he says, "He who has ears, let him hear." Why does he say something so similar, so close to each other?

The explanation of the parable is found several verses beyond the telling of the parable. Jesus had to go down a rabbit trail with his disciples, to explain why he was teaching with parables, and then he picks back up with the explanation of the parable in verse 18. To see why parables are used, see page i.

## Explanation of the Parable

### 📖 Matthew 13:19

_____

_____

_____

## This good news is received in four ways

1. _____

2. _____

3. _____

4. _____

Symbolically, the four soils describe the typical reaction from any one sinner who might hear the gospel of salvation.

1. _____

2. _____

3. _____

4. _____

---

*"Since salvation is by grace through faith (Ephesians 2:8) and grace-faith-salvation is a gift of God, any of the first three types of soil may become the fourth type of soil.*

*Those who choose to believe do so because they have received God's gift of grace-faith-salvation."[1]*

---

[1] (J. D. Quiggle, A Private Commentary on the Bible: Matthew's Gospel 2017)

# WHOSOEVER WILL

Lyrics and Melody by: Phillip P. Bliss;1838-1876

This hymn is in the public domain

1. "Whosoever heareth," shout, shout the sound!
Spread the blessed tidings all the world around:
Tell the joyful news wherever man is found,
"Whosoever will may come."

"Whosoever will, whosoever will!"
Send the proclamation over vale and hill;
"Tis a loving Father calls the wand'rer home:
"Whosoever will may come."

2. "Whosoever cometh need not delay,
Now the door is open, enter while you may;
Jesus is the true, the only Living Way:
"Whosoever will may come."

"Whosoever will, whosoever will!"
Send the proclamation over vale and hill;
"Tis a loving Father calls the wand'rer home:
"Whosoever will may come."

3. "Whosoever will" the promise is secure;
"Whosoever will," forever just endure;
"Whosoever will!" 'tis life forever more;
"Whosoever will may come."

"Whosoever will, whosoever will!"
Send the proclamation over vale and hill;
"Tis a loving Father calls the wand'rer home:
"Whosoever will may come."

# Chapter Nine

## *The Seed Growing Secretly*
Mark 4:26–29

*Figure 3 - Photo found on Google Images*

### Mark 4:26–29

**Who are the characters or items in this parable?**

_____

**When is the story told?**

_____

**Where is the story told?**

_____

**Who is in the audience?**

_____

_____

_____

_____

_____

## Application

_____

_____

_____

*God has not forgotten his promise of a mature kingdom.*

*Our timetable is just not His.*

---

### 2 Peter 3:8 (NLT)

"But you must not forget this one thing, dear friends: A day is like a thousand years to the Lord, and a thousand years is like a day."

# IN HIS TIME

Ecclesiastes 3:11 (NLT)

Yet God has made everything beautiful for its own time. He has planted eternity in the human heart, but even so, people cannot see the whole scope of God's work from beginning to end.

In His time, in His time,

He makes all things beautiful, in His time,

Lord, please show me everyday,

As You're teaching me Your way,

That You do just what You say, in Your time.

In Your time, in Your time,

You make all things beautiful, in Your time.

Lord, my life to Your I bring,

May each song I have to sing,

Be to You a lovely thing, in Your time.

By Maranatha! Music

# Chapter 10

## *The Sower, the Wheat, and the Weeds*
Matthew 13:24–29; Matthew 13:36–43

*Figure 4 - Photo found on Google Images*

📖 **Matthew 13:24–29**

**Who are the characters or items in this parable?**

_____

**When is the story told?**

_____

**Where is the story told?**

_____

**Who is in the audience?**

_____

## The Parable

_____

_____

_____

_____

_____

"Darnel [L. temulentum] usually grows in the same production zones as wheat and was a serious weed of cultivation until modern sorting machinery enabled darnel seeds to be separated efficiently from the wheat seed. The similarity between these two plants is so great that in some regions darnel is referred to as 'false wheat.' It bears a close resemblance to wheat until the ear appears. The spikes of L. temulentum are more slender than those of wheat. The spikelets are oriented edgeways to the rachis and have only a single glume, while those of wheat are oriented with the flat side to the rachis and have two glumes. The wheat will also appear brown when ripe, whereas the darnel is black."

*https://en.wikipedia.org/wiki/Lolium_temulentum*

## The Explanation

### 📖 Matthew 13:36–43

_____

_____

_____

☕ Christ is not addressing the church, but Jewish men seeking to understand the messianic kingdom. In their mind Christ is explaining the Davidic Messianic Kingdom, the *Thousand Year Reign*, to be established after Messiah's second advent.

### 📖 Matthew 13:43

*"The physical act of hearing is not sufficient. It is more important to take in what is heard, to comprehend it, and to assimilate it."* [1]

---

[1] (Morris, The Gospel according to Matthew (The Pillar New Testament Commentary) [1992])

## Summary

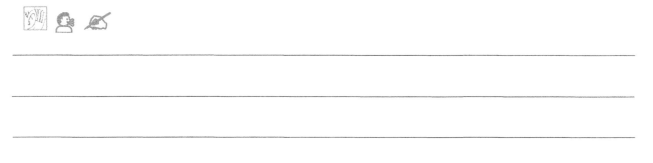

---

---

---

---

## A Challenge

From John Calvin,

"We ought to draw from this a useful admonition, not to become indolent and careless on account of our being surrounded by so many *stumbling–blocks*, but to be zealous and active in guarding against them...It is difficult, I admit, not to stumble frequently, and even sometimes to fall, when *stumbling–blocks* without number lie across our path.  But our minds ought to be fortified with confidence; for the Son of God, who commands his followers to walk in the midst of *stumbling blocks*, will unquestionably give us strength to overcome them all."

(Calvin, Commentary on a Harmony of the Evangelists Originally printed 1610 in London, England)

 Read Appendix Three for more information on John Calvin.

# Chapter Eleven

## *The Mustard Seed*
Matthew 13:31–32; Mark 4:30–32; Luke 13:18–19

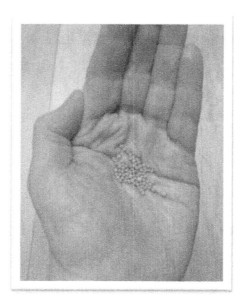

 📖 **Matthew 13:31–32**  📖 **Mark 4:30–32**  📖 **Luke 13:18–19**

**Who are the characters or items in this parable?**

_____

**When is the story told?**

_____

**Where is the story told?**

_____

**Who is in the audience?**

_____

# Do some research and learn about the mustard plant.

_____

_____

_____

_____

_____

_____

> *"Skeptics point out that the mustard is not the smallest of all seeds. Those with faith understand Jesus is speaking phenomenally, not scientifically. The mustard seed was the smallest seed planted and harvested by the agrarian population."* [1]

## What Is The Point Of This Parable, What Does it Mean?

_____

_____

_____

_____

_____

---

[1] (J. D. Quiggle, A Private Commentary on the Bible: Matthew's Gospel 2017)

**Photos found on Google images**

# Chapter Twelve

## *The Leaven*
Matthew 13:33; Luke 13:20

### 📖 **Matthew 13:33** 📖 **Luke 13:20**

**Who are the characters or items in this parable?**

_____

**When is the story told?**

_____

**Where is the story told?**

_____

 **Who is in the audience?**

_____

# What is Leaven and How Does It Work?

_____

_____

_____

## Create a Historical Word Picture

_____

_____

_____

_____

_____

*The action of leaven (and yeast) is to introduce gas (carbon dioxide) into the dough by breaking down the sugars found in grain. This chemical reaction makes the dough rise, gives it flavor, and gives it a light and airy texture.*

## What is the Application of This Parable?

_____

_____

_____

_____

*Just like the parable of the mustard seed, this parable shows the contrast and the cohesion between the small beginnings of the kingdom and its great end.*

# Chapter Thirteen

## *Three Short Parables*
## *About the Kingdom of Heaven*
### Matthew 13:44–50

Matthew records these three little parables, each of which starts with "the kingdom of heaven is like—The first two stress the value of the kingdom and obtaining membership into it. The third is about the finality of the separation that will take place at the end of this age if you do not lay hold of the kingdom while you are still living.

## Parable One – A Hidden Treasure

### 📖 **Matthew 13:44**

☕ In some writings, treasure might indicate the place where valuables are kept, but in this parable it is the thing itself that has value.

## Create a Historical Word Picture

_____

_____

_____

_____

**When this man found this hidden treasure, he hid it again.  Why?**

_____

_____

_____

## What Is The Point Of This Parable?

_____

_____

_____

## Parable Two – The Pearl

📖 **Matthew 13:45**

"Again…"

_____

_____

**What is the main difference between the two parables: The Hidden Treasure and a Pearl?**

_____

_____

## What is the Application for Us?

---

---

> "Again we see that it is well to take decisive action while the opportunity is there, and that no cost is too great when it is a matter of gaining the kingdom. The sacrifice of all that a man has is not too much. But in this second parable there is the further point that, whereas the man with the treasure could sell part of it and still be wealthy, the man with the pearl must retain it; his delight was in possessing it, not in the profit he could make from it."
>
> (Morris, The Gospel according to Matthew, [1992])

## Parable Three – The Fishing Net

### 📖 Matthew 13:47–50

**How is the message of this parable similar to the parable of wheat and tares?**

---

---

---

**How is it different from the parable of The Hidden Treasure and A Pearl?**

_____

_____

_____

**What is this parable trying to tell us?**

_____

_____

_____

# Chapter Fourteen

## *The Lost Sheep and The Lost Coin*
### Matthew 18:12–14 and Luke 15:3–10

At the beginning of the Davidic Messianic Kingdom, Gentiles and national ethnic Israel will be judged to determine who will enter the Kingdom. Those failing the judgment (those having the mark of the beast, Revelation 14:9–11) will go into hades to await the Great White Throne judgement (GWT). During the Kingdom there will be saved and unsaved throughout the Kingdom, with the unsaved going into hades upon their physical death. At the end of the Kingdom, Revelation 20:7–10, those living sinners who rebel against Christ will be killed and go into hades. Then the GWT will be conducted, the result of which is all the unsaved souls will be taken out of hades, rejoined with their resurrected (but corruptible) bodies,, and imprisoned in the lake of fire for eternity. Apparently the angels have some duties at the GWT, "The angels will go out and will separate the evil from among the righteous, and will cast them into the furnace of the fire."

*(J. D. Quiggle, A Private Commentary on the Bible: Matthew's Gospel 2017)*

## Prelude to Parable

### 📖 Matthew 18:10–11

*\*NOTE:  Some manuscripts add verse 11: For the Son of Man came to save the lost and others do not.*

### 📖 Matthew 18:10

**See** _____

**Do not** _____

**Despise** _____

**Who are 'These Little Ones?'** _____

_____

## 📖 Matthew 18:10b (ESV)

*10b "For I tell you that in heaven their angels always see the face of my Father who is in heaven."*

**What does the term, "their angels" mean?**

_____

_____

_____

*For a further discussion on angels read the book, Angelology, a True History of Angels by James D. Quiggle. This book can be found on Amazon in either print or digital format.*

## The Lost Sheep

## 📖 Matthew 18:12–14   📖 Luke 15:3–7

**Who are the characters or items in this parable?**

_____

**When is the story told?**

_____

**Where is the story told?**

_____

**Who is in the audience?**

_____

**Why does Jesus tell this parable?**

**What question or attitude is he addressing?**

_____

_____

_____

_____

## Matthew's Account of The Lost Sheep

### 📖 **Matthew 18:12–14.**

_____

_____

_____

_____

## Matthew's Application

_____

## Luke's Account of the Lost Sheep

 **Luke 15:5–7**

## Luke's Application

Figure 5 – Photo found on Google Images

## A Comparison of the Two Parables

| MATTHEW | LUKE |
|---|---|
|  |  |
|  |  |
|  |  |
|  |  |
|  |  |

## Transition to the Lost Coin Parable

📖 **Luke 15:7**

_____

_____

_____

**Why does Jesus tell another parable about something lost right after his story of the lost sheep?**

_____

_____

**What are the differences between a lost coin and a lost sheep?**

_____

_____

## The Lost Coin

📖 **Luke 15:8–10**

**Who are the characters or items in this parable?**

_____

**When is the story told?**

_____

**Where is the story told?**

_____

**Who is in the audience?**

_____

What might the coins represent to the woman?

_____

_____

**What was the woman's house like?**

_____

_____

**What happens when she finds the coin?**

_____

_____

## Application

📖 **Luke 15:10**

_____

_____

*True evangelism is grounded in the true joy of rescuing that which is totally lost.*

# He's Been Faithful

### Verse 1
In my moments of Fear
Through Every Pain Every Tear
There's A God Who's Been Faithful To Me
When My Strength Was All Gone
When My Heart Had No Song
Still In Love He's Proved Faithful To Me
Every Word He's Promised Is True
What I Thought Was Impossible I See My God Do

### Chorus
He's Been Faithful, Faithful To Me
Looking Back, His Love And Mercy I See
Though In My Heart I Have Questioned
even Failed To Believe He's Been Faithful, Faithful To Me

### Verse 2
When My Heart Looked Away The Many Times I Could Not Pray
Still My God- He Was Faithful To Me The Days I Spent So Selfishly
Reaching Out For What Pleased Me even Then God Was Faithful To Me
Every Time I Come Back To Him He Is Waiting with Open Arms
And I See Once Again

### Chorus
He's Been Faithful, Faithful To Me
Looking Back, His Love And Mercy I See
Though In My Heart I Have Questioned
even Failed To Believe He's Been Faithful, Faithful To Me

**Songwriter:** CAROL CYMBALA

# Chapter Fifteen

## *The Unforgiving Slave*
Matthew 18:23–34

## 📖 Matthew 18:21–35

**Who are the characters or items in this parable?**

_____

**When is the story told?**

_____

**Where is the story told?**

_____

**Who is in the audience?**

_____

_____

_____

_____

## What is a Denarii?  What is a Talent?

_____

_____

### 📖 **Matthew 18:25**

**Why were the slave's family put in prison?**

_____

_____

**How long would it take this slave to pay back the Master?**

_____

_____

### 📖 **Matthew 18:26–27**

**What did the slave do?**

_____

_____

**What was the master's response?**

_____

_____

_____

_____

_____

## 📖 Matthew 18:28–30

👂 🗣 ✍

**What do these verses tell us about the slave's character?**

_____

_____

_____

_____

## 📖 Matthew 18:31

👂 🗣 ✍

**Give this verse a title.  Why did you make this choice?**

_____

_____

## You Wicked Slave

## 📖 Matthew 18:32–34

👂 🗣 ✍

_____

_____

_____

## The Application

📖 **Matthew 18:35**

_____

_____

_____

_____

# Grace, Greater than Our Sin

Julia H. Johnston - 1911

### Verse 1:

Marvelous grace of our loving Lord,
Grace that exceeds our sin and our guilt!
Yonder on Calvary's mount outpoured,
There where the blood of the Lamb was spilled.

### Refrain:

Grace, grace, God's grace,
Grace that will pardon and cleanse within;
Grace, grace, God's grace,
Grace that is greater than all our sin!

### Verse 3:

Dark is the stain that we cannot hide;
What can we do to wash it away?
Look! There is flowing a crimson tide,
Brighter than snow you may be today.
*Repeat Refrain*

### Verse 2:

Sin and despair, like the sea waves cold,
Threaten the soul with infinite loss;
Grace that is greater, yes, grace untold,
Points to the refuge, the mighty cross.
*Repeat Refrain*

### Verse 4:

Marvelous, infinite, matchless grace,
Freely bestowed on all who believe!
You that are longing to see His face,
Will you this moment His grace receive?
*Repeat Refrain*

# Chapter Sixteen

## *The Sheep, the Door, and the Good Shepherd*
John 10:1–30

*Figure 6 - https://www.aloha-friday.org/archives/5974*

## Parable 1

### 📖 John 10:1–18

**Who are the characters or items in parable one?**

_____

**When is the story told?**

_____

**Where is the story told?**

_____

**Who is in the audience?**

_____

_____

_____

_____

To demonstrate this extraordinary concept of "abiding," Jesus proceeds to tell the parables of the Shepherd and His Sheep.

## John 10:1a

*1a "Truly, truly, I say to you..." Or "Amen, amen, I say to you."*

Figure 7 - Pictures of sheepfolds found on Google Images

## The Sheepfold

*1b ... he who does not enter the sheepfold"*

## What is a sheepfold?  What was its purpose?

Figure 8 – Pictures of sheepfolds found on Google Images

> "Important to our understanding of the discourse is the knowledge that domesticated sheep truly need a shepherd. Sheep can overgraze a field. Their bite cuts off the grass at ground level, unlike other animals whose bite leaves short blades for regrowth. Sheep will drink any water, whether fresh, stagnate, or poisoned. Sheep will wander into dangerous territory, fall off steep hills or cliffs, scatter when threatened by a predator, over–eat and become sick, or over–heat and not seek shelter. Domesticated sheep are woolly eating machines that have come to depend on man for their welfare and as a result have minimal survival skills. Without the shepherd the sheep were helpless."
>
> *(J. D. Quiggle, A Private Commentary On the Bible: John 1–12 2014)*

---

*"He [Jesus] is saying that my life is a sheepfold to which He alone, the Good Shepherd, is the rightful owner."1*

---

## A Thief and a Robber

### 📖 John 10:1

---

## The Shepherd

### 📖 John 10:2

---

1 (Keller, The Shepherd Triology: A Sheperd Looks at the Good Shepherd 1996)

## The Gate Keeper

📖 **John 10:3a**

## The Sheep

📖 **John 10:3b–5**

**How do the shepherds collect just <u>their</u> sheep?**

**How do the sheep know their shepherd's voice?**

**Compare the differences between how sheep are raised in the Middle East versus in most of North America?**

_____

_____

_____

**What is the application between Jesus and his servants/believers?**

_____

_____

## I Am the Door

### 📖 John 10:7

**What is the function of a door or gate in a sheepfold?  Why does Jesus call himself the "door"?**

_____

_____

_____

_____

### 📖 John 10:8

**What does the word "all" mean in this verse?**

_____

**Who were the "all"?**

_____

**Who were NOT the "all"?**

In this second phase of the parable Jesus proceeds to elaborate in great detail on what it means for a man or woman to enter into His life. "By that is implied the way whereby we come into His care, enjoy His management, and revel in the abundance of His life shared with us in gracious generosity. Again it must be emphasized that His audience did not really understand Him. When He completes teaching them, they charged Him with being insane, possessed of an evil spirit, and unworthy of a hearing." [2]

📖 **John 10:9–10a**

## The Good Shepherd

📖 **John 10:10b–11**

---

[2] (Keller, The Shepherd Triology: A Sheperd Looks at the Good Shepherd 1996)

## The Hired Hand

📖 **John 10:12–13**

"Jesus uses these facts of life to communicate a spiritual truth. Jesus has a sheepfold where he keeps his sheep. Since he is the door, then those sheep which enter into his sheepfold through Jesus-the-door are his sheep, always and forever. They will go in and out of the sheepfold through Jesus-the-door and find pasture. In their going in and out they never cease to be his sheep. Looking ahead to v. 11, when the sheep go in and out the door, Jesus goes with them: he is not only the door of the sheep but the shepherd of the sheep. We must take care not to make the illustration teach every doctrine relating to salvation. What is in view here, the main point, is that Jesus himself makes a sinner his sheep, and then he keeps his sheep secure at all times and places. Sinners seeking salvation enter into salvation through faith in Jesus as their Savior, and then they become his sheep and he becomes their shepherd."

*(J. D. Quiggle, A Private Commentary on the Bible: John 1–12 2014)*

*"Oh, the wonder and joy of being known by God! The strength and consolation of being in the care of Christ who fully and completely understands us! Such awareness and such knowing stills our spirits, soothes our souls, and fills us with quiet awe.*

*'O God, You do know me through and through.'"[3]*

## 📖 *John 10:14–15*

## What are Characteristics of a Good Shepherd?

_____

_____

_____

> "We in the western world have become extremely skilled at living behind a false façade. We wear masks. Seldom do we disclose our true identity. We try to present a brave front to the world, even though within we may be shattered, broken people. We proceed on the assumption that most people really don't know us and don't care. We often run a bluff on others, based on the premise that they will not or cannot be bothered to really find us out.
>
> "The net result is that for many, life becomes a sham. It is almost playacting. It is played by people playing little games with each other. Much of it is really make-believe. It lacks depth, honesty, or sincerity. People become phonies, they are riddled with skepticism and cynicism. They really don't know where they are at.
>
> "Against this background of confused and bewildered life God steps onto the stage and states dramatically, surely, and without apology, 'I know you! I understand you! I have known all about you all the time!'"
>
> *(Keller, The Shepherd Triology: A Sheperd Looks at the Good Shepherd 1996)*

---

[3] (Keller, The Shepherd Triology: A Sheperd Looks at the Good Shepherd 1996)

## With your class think, talk, and answer these questions based on the above quote.

Does it give you comfort that God knows you?

_____

Does it bother you and make you uncomfortable that God knows you?

_____

What does God know about you? (get really detailed)

_____

What happens us when we really get a grasp on this "knowing" thing God has for us?  How might it transform our lives?

_____

Psalm 139:1-14

1 O Lord, you have examined my heart and know everything about me.

2 You know when I sit down or stand up. You know my thoughts even when I'm far away.

3 You see me when I travel and when I rest at home. You know everything I do.

4 You know what I am going to say even before I say it, Lord.

5 You go before me and follow me. You place your hand of blessing on my head.

6 Such knowledge is too wonderful for me, too great for me to understand!

7 I can never escape from your Spirit! I can never get away from your presence!

8 If I go up to heaven, you are there; if I go down to the grave, you are there.

9 If I ride the wings of the morning, if I dwell by the farthest oceans, 10 even there your hand will guide me, and your strength will support me.

11 I could ask the darkness to hide me and the light around me to become night— 12but even in darkness I cannot hide from you. To you the night shines as bright as day. Darkness and light are the same to you.

13 You made all the delicate, inner parts of my body and knit me together in my mother's womb.

14 Thank you for making me so wonderfully complex! Your workmanship is marvelous—how well I know it.

## The Father and The Son

### 📖 John 10:15–16

_____

_____

_____

"In v. 16 the reference to 'this fold' must be to the lost sheep of the house of Israel to whom Jesus was currently ministering. Jesus will call his sheep out of the sheepfold of Israel, and the sheep that remain in Israel are not his sheep. There is another sheepfold, not of Israel, and Jesus will call his other sheep out of that other sheepfold. The 'other sheep' cannot be the house of Israel but are the lost sheep of the Gentile house. Christ will call his Gentile sheep and they will hear his voice and follow him (the words 'other sheep I have' show they already belong to Jesus). Then there will be, not a Jewish church and a Gentile church, but one flock under one shepherd. These truths are reflected in two passages outside the Gospels, one in Hebrews and one in Ephesians. At Hebrews 3:5 Moses is said to have been faithful in all his house. Moses' house was the fold of Israel; but Christ is faithful over the whole house, 'whose house we are' says the Writer of Hebrews. The house of Christ contains all believers from the Hebrew and Gentile folds. Christ's house is the one flock of believers in Christ as Savior.

"In Ephesians 2:11–22, Paul tells the saved Ephesian Gentiles that they and the saved Hebrews together form one "household of God." The new flock Jesus will create from Israel and the Gentiles—the New Testament church—is not another room in the house of Israel, but is a new house with one room, the house and room of the New Testament saved, who are those who hear and follow Jesus. 'For [Christ's] sheep have a sheepfold, which is expounded to be the church, as may be gathered from John 10:16.'

"However, let us be clear that "the unity of the flock is determined by a common following of the one shepherd [Jesus], not by the erection of a single outward organization."

*(J. D. Quiggle, A Private Commentary On the Bible: John 1–12 2014)*

# 📖 John 10:17–18

> "The subject that connects vv. 17–18 to the discourse is the theme of Jesus laying down his life for the sheep, vv. 11, 15. The Father loves Jesus because he lays down his life to save the sheep from their sins. The Father doesn't love the Son just because he lays down his life for the sheep—he is not withholding his love until Jesus lays down his life for the sheep! The Father has loved, presently loves, and always will love the Son, John 5:20. What is in view is not the essential love of God the Father for God the Son, but the Father's approval of the Son in his office of Redeemer-Savior-Mediator between God and man. What is in view is the voluntary obedience of the Savior toward the Father and his complete dependence on him, which expresses the Son's love for the Father, a love which is reciprocated by the Father. Theirs is a mutual love not caused by certain acts but expressed in acts... So the Father loves the Son, and because of his love gives the Son the authority to lay down his life to save the sheep, and take it up again to shepherd the sheep. The reference is to Jesus' death and resurrection. The important point is not the salvation of the sheep, but the authority given Jesus to save the sheep through his death and resurrection."
>
> *(J. D. Quiggle, A Private Commentary On the Bible: John 1–12 2014)*

## Parable 2 – Christ in Me and Me in Christ

### John 10:25–30.

**Who are the characters or items in this parable?**

_____

**When is the story told?**

_____

**Where is the story told?**

_____

**Who is in the audience?**

_____

Several months have passed between the Feast of Tabernacles (Autumn) and the Feast of Dedication (Winter). Jesus was in Jerusalem to participate in the Feast of Dedication; it was a joyous celebration with its festive candles. (This feast was celebrated in the home as well as in the Temple)

### John 10:25

_____

_____

_____

---

*Jesus was the Christ; he simply wasn't the Christ they were looking for.*

---

📖 Isaiah 61:1–3; John 10:26b–27

"The outcome of the confrontation is plain: they 'The Jews', did not believe. Was their unbelief the cause, or the result, of their status of 'not being Jesus' sheep?' Jesus through John answers their question."[1]

📖 📖 👤 ✍

John 1:12 _____

John 5:21 _____

John 6:37 _____

John 6:44 _____

Acts 16:31 _____

Ephesians 2:8–9 _____

---

[1] (J. D. Quiggle, A Private Commentary On the Bible: John 1-12 2014)

None of these verses indicate that a sinner <u>cannot</u> be saved.  However, the sinner also has a responsibility in being saved.  The sinner must respond to the Spirit's conviction of sin and then the sinner must seek Jesus as Savior and receive him by faith.

The truly important thing is that, 'The Shepherd' knows his sheep. Based on verses 27 and 28 what are six characteristics of a true  believer (a sheep of Jesus).

1. _____

2. _____

3. _____

4. _____

5. _____

6. _____

_____

_____

_____

_____

## 📖 John 10:29–30.

**In an online dictionary look up the words "snatch" and "taken" and define them.**

_____

_____

_____

**Look up the words in Strong's Concordance and define what the Greek says.**

_____

_____

**Look up these words in a Bible Dictionary and define them.**

_____

_____

_____

_____

_____

- The intentions of God toward His own is ALWAYS GOOD.

- He only has our best interests at heart.

- His desires are only for our well–being.

- He is the Shepherd who has enormous good will and deep compassion for the sheep/people of His pasture.

- How comforting to know that we don't have to hold on to Him but that He has a hold on us. We simply need to rest in the quiet assurance of being in his hands.

*He told them plainly, but they rejected Him.*

*The majority of people still reject the Good Shepherd.*

*Yet to those who hear His voice, respond to His call, come under His care, and follow Him, the commitments of The Shepherd to his sheep come to fruition.*

*His Sheep, His People – they will find life, overflowing life, fulfilling life, abiding life, eternal life, forever in His presence. Life in Christ and Christ in them.*

I suggest closing this study with the song, *"The Good Shepherd"* (Chapter 10) – The Book of John in Song by The Tommy Walker Ministries. (http://www.tommywalkerministries.org)  A link to their performance can be found on YouTube:
https://www.youtube.com/watch?v=TYKRdKwYVQI

# Chapter Seventeen

## *The Samaritan Who Was a Friend*
Luke 10:25–37

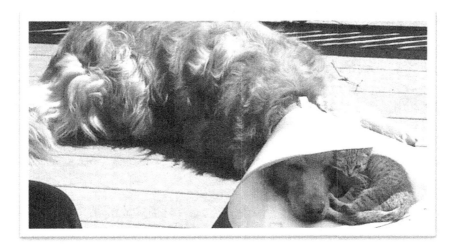

*Figure 9 - Photo found on Google Images*

## 📖 Luke 10:25–37 (HCSB)

*25 "Just then an expert in the law stood up to test Him, saying, 'Teacher, what must I do to inherit eternal life?'*

## The First Question, asked by Jesus
*26 'What is written in the law?' He asked him. 'How do you read it?'*

*27 He answered: 'Love the Lord your God with all your heart, with all your soul, with all your strength, and with all your mind; and your neighbor as yourself.'*

## Confirmation of answer by Jesus
*28 'You've answered correctly,' He told him. 'Do this and you will live.'*

*29 But wanting to justify himself, he asked Jesus, 'And who is my neighbor?'*

## The Second Answer, by Jesus by way of a Parable
*30 Jesus took up the question and said: 'A man was going down from Jerusalem to Jericho and fell into the hands of robbers. They stripped him, beat him up, and fled, leaving him half dead. 31 A priest happened to be going down that road. When he saw him, he passed by on the other side. 32 In the same way, a Levite, when he arrived at the place and saw him, passed by on the other side. 33 But a Samaritan on his journey came up to him, and when he saw the man, he had compassion. 34 He went over to him and bandaged his wounds, pouring on olive oil and wine. Then he put him on his own animal, brought him to an inn, and took care of him. 35 The next day he took out two denarii, gave them to the innkeeper, and said, 'Take care of him. When I come back I'll reimburse you for whatever extra you spend.'*

## The Third Question, asked by Jesus
*36 'Which of these three do you think proved to be a neighbor to the man who fell into the hands of the robbers?'*

*37 'The one who showed mercy to him,' he said.*

## Confirmation of answer by Jesus
*"Then Jesus told him, 'Go and do the same.'"*

**Who are the characters or items in this parable?**

_____

**When is the story told?**

_____

**Where is the story told?**

_____

 **Who is in the audience?**

_____

_____

_____

_____

**In an online dictionary look up the word "inherit" and define.**

_____

_____

**Look up the word "inherit" in Strong's Concordance and define what the Greek says.**

_____

_____

**Look up the word "inherit" in a Bible Dictionary and define.**

_____

_____

_____

_____

_____

_____

_____

_____

## 📖 Luke 10:27

_____

_____

_____

_____

Leviticus 19:9-18 (ESV)

**Love Your Neighbor as Yourself**

9 When you reap the harvest of your land, you shall not reap your field right up to its edge, neither shall you gather the gleanings after your harvest. 10 And you shall not strip your vineyard bare, neither shall you gather the fallen grapes of your vineyard. You shall leave them for the poor and for the sojourner: I am the Lord your God.

11 You shall not steal; you shall not deal falsely; you shall not lie to one another. 12 You shall not swear by my name falsely, and so profane the name of your God: I am the Lord.

13 You shall not oppress your neighbor or rob him. The wages of a hired worker shall not remain with you all night until the morning. 14 You shall not curse the deaf or put a stumbling block before the blind, but you shall fear your God: I am the Lord.

15 You shall do no injustice in court. You shall not be partial to the poor or defer to the great, but in righteousness shall you judge your neighbor. 16 You shall not go around as a slanderer among your people, and you shall not stand up against the life of your neighbor: I am the Lord.

17 You shall not hate your brother in your heart, but you shall reason frankly with your neighbor, lest you incur sin because of him. 18 You shall not take vengeance or bear a grudge against the sons of your own people, but you shall love your neighbor as yourself: I am the Lord.

## Luke 10:28

## 📖 Luke 10:29

_____

_____

_____

_____

## The Parable

## 📖 Luke 10:30–35

_____

_____

_____

_____

If you are hindered by a I–don't–want–to, a biased attitude, or a mindset of it–might–require–too–much–effort, you can always find an excuse to neglect a labor of love when it presents itself.

## 📖 Luke 10:36

The tables are turned once more. Jesus now makes the accuser answer his own question.

_____

_____

_____

_____

📖 **Luke 10:37**

_____

_____

_____

_____

_____

_____

Do you notice that he is unable to bring himself to answer, The Samaritan, but answers "The one.... "  Are we like that?

I suggest closing this study with this video/song I found on YouTube: *Who is My Neighbor?* https://www.youtube.com/watch?v=K5IAka0Ocj8

# Chapter Eighteen

## *A Friend in Need and How to Pray*
Luke 11:5–13

## Luke 11:1–13

**Who are the characters or items in this parable?**

_____

**When is the story told?**

_____

**Where is the story told?**

_____

**Who is in the audience?**

_____

*The model prayer that Jesus just taught his disciples does not address the attitude that one should have when engaging in prayer. Jesus now uses a parable to communicate the attitude. Jesus shows us that God is amicable and that we should approach him often and with boldness.*

## A.D. 1 Is Different From A.D. 2019

Using online sources or books available to you, learn and then discuss just how different A.D. 1 is from A.D. 2019. (Make sure you touch on cultural norms as part of this discussion.)

_____

_____

_____

_____

_____

_____

_____

## 📖 Luke 11:9–10

In these verses Jesus is explaining that we are on an adventure with God; ask, seek, knock. What do these words mean?

- **Ask:** _____

- **Seek:** _____

- **Knock:** _____

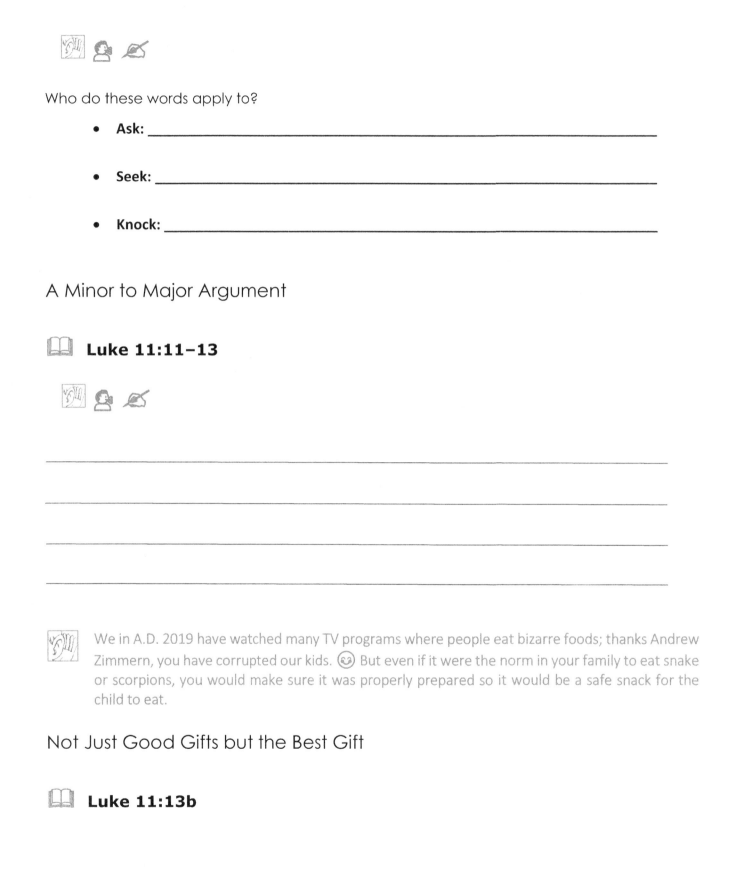

Who do these words apply to?

- **Ask:** _____

- **Seek:** _____

- **Knock:** _____

## A Minor to Major Argument

📖 **Luke 11:11–13**

_____

_____

_____

_____

We in A.D. 2019 have watched many TV programs where people eat bizarre foods; thanks Andrew Zimmern, you have corrupted our kids. 😊 But even if it were the norm in your family to eat snake or scorpions, you would make sure it was properly prepared so it would be a safe snack for the child to eat.

## Not Just Good Gifts but the Best Gift

📖 **Luke 11:13b**

_____

_____

*We as humans give essential and good things to our children.*

*But God will not even withhold his very best gift, the Holy Spirit, from his sons and daughters.  It is not that the Holy Spirit is a substitute for all our other needs, but rather that, the gift of the Holy Spirit as the best and highest gift, is an example of the minor–to–major argument.*

*The receiving of the best gift, the Holy Spirit (Major), should give us constant assurance that he will not withhold from us anything that we need (Minor).*

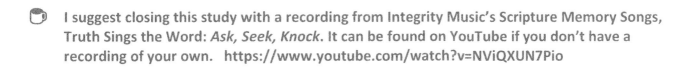

I suggest closing this study with a recording from Integrity Music's Scripture Memory Songs, Truth Sings the Word: *Ask, Seek, Knock*. It can be found on YouTube if you don't have a recording of your own.  https://www.youtube.com/watch?v=NViQXUN7Pio

# Chapter Nineteen

## *Foolishly Preoccupied*
Luke 12:13–23

*Figure 10 - https://www.thebarnyardstore.com/blog/detail/?id=322*

## Luke 12:13–23

**Who are the characters or items in this parable?**

_____

**When is the story told?**

_____

**Where is the story told?**

_____

**Who is in the audience?**

_____

**What had Jesus been teaching about earlier in Luke 12?**

1. _____

2. _____

3. _____

4. _____

## 📖 Luke 12:13

Why did this man get up and ask his question?

👤 ✍️

---

## 📖 Luke 12:14–15

🔊 👤 ✍️

---

---

# Greed and Coveting

## 📖 Luke 12:16

🔊 👤 ✍️

---

---

---

## 📖 Luke 12:17–19

> "I": Strong's word 1473: *egó*: I, the first-person pronoun.
>
> "My": Strong's word 1700: *emoú* ("mine, my") then is an "emphasized possessive."
>
> *(Strong n.d.)*

**In verses 17–19 how many times does egó and emoú occur?**

_____

_____

**What does the old testament say about having and having not?**

📖   Deuteronomy 15:11

_____

_____

_____

## But God

📖 **Luke 12:20**

*In Ephesians 4:2 we see a "But God" where God intervenes with mercy.*

*The "But God," in Luke 12:20 is not of the same quality.  In this parable God bursts on the scene of this man who is filled with self–satisfaction and calls the rich farmer a fool.*

_____

_____

## Luke 12:21a

_____

_____

## The Application To The Multitude

## Luke 21:21b

**Does Jesus condemn owning stuff?** _____

**What is it that he is disapproving of?** _____

**What is a correct view of the stuff we own?** _____

_____

What application is there for your life?

_____

_____

**Matthew 6:19-21 (NLT)**

19 "Don't store up treasures here on earth, where moths eat them and rust destroys them, and where thieves break in and steal. 20 Store your treasures in heaven, where moths and rust cannot destroy, and thieves do not break in and steal. 21 Where your treasure is, there the desires of your heart will also be."

# The Author's Closing Remarks

The eternal life of the believer is not just unending physical or spiritual life, it is also life in God's home, in His presence, for eternity.

To be fit to live in God's presence is to possess the qualities of sinlessness, righteousness, and holiness.

The believer gains those qualities, and therefore can live in God's presence. How? Because he is "in Christ," which means he participates in the eternal life of which Christ is the origin and source.

If you do not know Christ as your savior you are not "in Christ" and you will not participate in that eternal life in the presence of God.

But!

God has intervened so that you can be "in Christ."

### Ephesians 2:4–5

4 But God, being rich in mercy, because of the great love with which he loved us, 5 even when we were dead in our trespasses, made us alive together with Christ—by grace you have been saved

### John 3:16 (ESV)

16 "For God so loved the world, that he gave his only Son, that whoever believes in him should not perish but have eternal life.

The Apostle Paul in the book of Romans lays out what has become known as "The Roman's Road" to salvation.

1) We are born lost in sin:

### Romans 3:23 (ESV)

23 "For all have sinned and fall short of the glory of God."

### Romans 3:10–18 (ESV)

10 "as it is written: None is righteous, no, not one; 11 no one understands; no one seeks for God. 12 All have turned aside; together they have become worthless; no one does good, not even one. 13 Their throat is an open grave; they use their tongues to deceive. The venom of asps is under their lips. 14 Their mouth is full of curses and bitterness. 15 Their feet are swift to shed blood; 16 in their paths are ruin and misery, 17 and the way of peace they have not known. 18 There is no fear of God before their eyes."

2) There are consequences of sin:

### Romans 6:23a (ESV)

23a "For the wages of sin is death,"

3) God's Gift (his reconciliation to Himself):

### Romans 6:23b (ESV)

23b "but the free gift of God is eternal life in Christ Jesus our Lord."

### Romans 5:8 (ESV)

8 "but God shows his love for us in that while we were still sinners, Christ died for us."

4) Confession is Required:

### Romans 10:9-10

9 because, if you confess with your mouth that Jesus is Lord and believe in your heart that God raised him from the dead, you will be saved. 10 For with the heart one believes and is justified, and with the mouth one confesses and is saved.

### Romans 10:13

13 For "everyone who calls on the name of the Lord will be saved."

### Ephesians 2:8-9

8 For by grace you have been saved through faith. And this is not your own doing; it is the gift of God, 9 not a result of works, so that no one may boast.

4) The Results of Salvation:

### Romans 5:1

5 "Therefore, since we have been justified by faith, we have peace with God through our Lord Jesus Christ."

### Romans 8:1

8 "There is therefore now no condemnation for those who are in Christ Jesus."

### Romans 8:38-39

38 For I am sure that neither death nor life, nor angels nor rulers, nor things present nor things to come, nor powers, [39] nor height nor depth, nor anything else in all creation, will be able to separate us from the love of God in Christ Jesus our Lord."

Would you like to experience salvation?

If so, you just need to pray a simple prayer to God in faith and believing the verses written above are true. There is a sample prayer on the next page.

Saying this prayer is a way to declare to God that you are relying on Jesus Christ's redemptive work for your salvation.

The printed words themselves will not save you. Even just saying them for the sake saying them will not save you. Only faith in Jesus Christ can provide salvation!

> God, I know that I am a sinner and deserve punishment.
>
> But Jesus Christ took that punishment, the punishment I deserved, so when I believe in Him because of his sacrifice on the cross and have faith that He paid for my sins, I will be forgiven.
>
> I am placing my trust in You for salvation.
>
> Thank You for Your forgiveness of my sin, and Your gift of eternal life! Amen!

1) If you have asked God to save you from your sins the next step is to find a Bible believing church where you can be discipled and grow in your Christian faith.

2) If you have asked God to save you or you are struggling with a decision contact me at:

   https://www.facebook.com/LindaQuiggleAuthor/

I would be privileged to share in this joyful salvific event with you or assist you in making that decision.

In Christ Alone,

*Linda M. Quiggle*

While you contemplate the words above, listen to this recording: I WILL POUR WATER by Rita King Chadwick. Video production by Jam Productions

https://www.youtube.com/watch?v=c-FsOiAjDFw&feature=youtu.be

# Appendix One

## Fig Trees – Sycamore Fig Trees

*Figure 1 -Sycamore bearing figs*

Information found on http://sharobim1.blogspot.com/

The fig tree is one of the oldest known fruit trees. Illustrations of fig trees are found on monuments and tombs of ancient Egypt. The Sycamore Fig grew in abundance along the Nile, the region from which Abraham's ancestors came (Zohary and Hopf, authors of Domestication of Plants in the Old World. Oxford University Press), assert that Egypt was 'the principal area of sycamore fig development.' They note "that the fruit and the timber, and sometimes even the twigs, are richly represented in the tombs of the Egyptian Early, Middle, and Late Kingdoms. In numerous cases the parched sycons bear characteristic gashing marks indicating that this art, which induces ripening, was practiced in Egypt in ancient times."

Some facts about the Sycamore Fig—taken from Wikipedia.

*Figure 2- Mature Sycamore Tree*

- Their leaves resemble those of a mulberry.
- Cultivated since early times.
- Grows naturally in Lebanon, naturalized in Egypt and Israel.
- Grows up to 60 ft. tall and 18 ft. wide, have heart shaped leaves.
- Fruit is a large edible fig, 2-3 cm in diameter, ripening from buff-green to yellow to orange. Born in thick clusters.
- The Sycamore fig (GEMEZE) in modern Egypt is mostly used as food for domestic animals.
- Near Orient—tree of great importance and used extensively, produces delightful shade.
- Ancient Egypt, called it: Tree of Life. The fruit and timber of the Sycamore Fig were found in Egyptian tombs.

In Egyptian iconography the Sycamore stands on the threshold of life and death, veiling the threshold by its abundant low-hanging foliage. Pharaohs called the Sycamore Fig, *Nehet*.

With one striking exception, the fig tree symbolizes life, prosperity, peace and righteousness throughout the Bible. Micah 4:4 reads: "But they shall sit every man under his vine and under his fig tree; and no one shall make them afraid."

*"Three crops of figs in Palestine.* The early figs, not very many in number, but large in size, are ripe a month before the main crop; the summer or main crop is ready in August and September; the winter figs remain on the trees until late in the fall of the year. . . . The summer crop that is not eaten as fresh fruit is dried on the housetops, and then used in the winter months."

*"The fig tree a sign of the season.* The fig tree shows sign of foliage later than some of the other fruit trees of Palestine. The unfolding of the fig leaves and the deepening of their color is thought of as a sign that summertime is at hand."

# Appendix Two

This is an excerpt from the book, *Dispensational Eschatology, An Explanation and Defense of the Doctrine* by James D. Quiggle.

## Dispensationalism

"A brief review of dispensational theology will be useful to later discussions of eschatology. In this chapter I will discuss dispensational theology, followed by chapters on the hermeneutics used by dispensationalism, the application of dispensational hermeneutics to eschatology, and a review of certain terms applicable to dispensational eschatology.

"There is no more primary problem in the whole matter of dispensationalism than that of definition. By this is meant not simply arriving at a single sentence definition of the word but also formulating a definition/description of the concept."[1] The goal of this chapter is to define and describe dispensationalism and its relation to certain aspects of biblical theology.

"To begin, one must distinguish between a "dispensation" and the systematic theology known as "dispensationalism." Failure to do so has often resulted in misunderstanding and prejudice against the theology. Most critics of dispensationalism define the theology by the AD 1909 *Scofield Reference Bible's* definition of a dispensation. However, just as other branches of theology have undergone systematization and development, e.g., the doctrines of God, salvation, Christ, the Holy Spirit, the church, etc., so too in eschatology and dispensationalism. When the doctrine of last things, which is eschatology, returned to the church's attention in the late 1800s, the Holy Spirit led certain leaders in that movement to discern the broad outlines of a theology that would determine how the church understood eschatology. As time has passed, the Spirit has given understanding of how the theology of dispensationalism interacts with the whole range of Bible doctrines.

## WHAT IS A DISPENSATION?

"Three Greek words are translated dispensation, steward, stewardship, administration, job, or commission (depending on the Bible version). The verb *oikonoméō*,[2] means to be a manager of a household. The noun *oikonómos*,[3] means a person who manages the domestic affairs of a family, business, or minor; an overseer, a steward, a house steward; a treasurer; the chamberlain of a city. The noun *oikonomía*,[4] describes the position, work, responsibility, or arrangement of an administration, as of

---

[1] Ryrie, *Dispensationalism*, 23.
[2] Zodhiates, *WSDNT*, s. v. "3621. *oikonoméō*."
[3] Ibid., s. v. "3623. *oikonómos*."
[4] Ibid., s. v. "3622. *oikonomía*."

a house or property, either one's own or another's.

"A dispensation is a stewardship, arrangement, or economy. This is how the dispensationalist and the Bible use the term. The Bible uses the term in this way in at least two verses. The first is Ephesians 1:10, "the *oikonomía* of the fullness of the times." The second is Ephesians 3:2, the *oikonomía* of the grace of God." Other uses of *oikonomía* are Luke 16:2, 3, 4; 1 Corinthians 9:17; Ephesians 3:9; Colossians 1:25; 1 Timothy 1:4. The verb *oikonoméō* is used at Luke 16:2 corresponding to the noun *oikonomía*. The word *oikonómos* is used at Luke 12:42; 16:1, 3, 8; Romans 16:23; 1 Corinthians 4:1, 2; Galatians 4:2; Titus 1:7; 1 Peter 4:10.

"The word "dispensation" as used by the Bible and dispensationalists, corresponds to the modern word "economy." In fact, "economy" is derived from the Greek *oikonomía* by way of the Latin *oeconomia* and the French *economie* (which first appeared about AD 1530). An "economy," in the sense the Bible uses the word "dispensation," corresponds to the more archaic use of the word, i.e., the management of household affairs. In more modern terms an economy is the management of resources, or the orderly interplay between parts of a system. All these definitions fit the dispensationalist's view of the world as the household of God, wherein he manages its resources— human beings—and the interplay of his plans and processes between all the parts, to bring him glory.

"Biblically, an "economy" has a twofold perspective. From God's point of view it is the administration of his affairs; from man's point of view it is the stewardship of his responsibilities in relation to God's revealed will. Since a dispensation is God's economy, we might define it as the way God works out his purpose in the world. This is in fact how Ryrie defines a dispensation:

A dispensation is a distinguishable economy in the outworking of God's purpose.[5]

In his book Ryrie names others who have come to the same conclusion.

"From time to time God changes his economy. A business or household manager will change his/her management practices to adapt to changing circumstances in the world. Even so, God changes the administration of his affairs, and thereby makes changes to man's stewardship responsibilities, by making changes in how God works out his purpose in the world. God's purpose doesn't change, but God changes his economies—his dispensations—to interact appropriately with humanity's development and changing circumstances.

Erich Sauer provides several observations that help define how God changes his economies. He wrote, "a new period [dispensation] always begins only when *from the side of God* a change is introduced in the composition of the principles valid up to that time; that is, when from the side of God three things concur:

A continuance of certain ordinances valid until then;

An annulment of other regulations until then valid;

A fresh introduction of new principles not before valid.[6]

"In other words, when God changes one economy for another, some ordinances (precepts,

---

[5] Ryrie, *Dispensationalism*, 28.
[6] Sauer, *Dawn*, 194.

regulations) from the preceding economy remain valid, other ordinances from the preceding economy are annulled, and new ordinances for the new economy are instituted.

Let us be clear. God does not change his economies because humanity has surprised him with some new development or circumstance. God knew what humanity would do (foreknowledge), because he created the universe and all its creatures to operate according to his purpose (foreordination). God's purpose never changes. His plans are designed to fulfill that purpose. God's dispensations are processes he has designed to accomplish his plans that fulfill his purpose. God's changing economies are pre-planned by his foreordination and foreknowledge to meet the changing circumstances of a developing humanity. (For an in-depth explanation of God's foreordination and foreknowledge, see my book *God's Choices*.)

"To understand what God is doing in his household, we begin with a discussion of the conditions applicable to the several dispensations.

## THE DISPENSATIONS

"I identify the several dispensations with reference to the prominent persons and events with whom a dispensation began and ended. These are:

Adam to Noah

Noah to Abraham

Abraham to Moses

Moses to Christ's resurrection

Christ's resurrection to rapture of the church

Rapture to Christ's second advent

Christ's Davidic-Messianic-Millennial reign to Christ the Judge at the Great White Throne Judgment.

The eternal state (God eternally face-to-face with saved mankind) following the GREAT WHITE THRONE

Certain dispensations might also be defined in terms of the covenants God made with mankind's representatives.

Adam to Noah (Adamic covenant)

Noah to Abraham, (Post-Flood Noahic covenant)

Abraham to Moses, (Abrahamic covenant)

Moses to Christ's resurrection (Mosaic, Palestinian, Davidic, and New covenants)

Christ's resurrection to rapture of the church (application of New covenant to individual Hebrews and Gentiles)

Christ's Davidic-Messianic-Millennial reign (fulfillment of Abrahamic, Davidic, Palestinian, and New covenants toward national ethnic Israel)

"As may be seen from both lists, dispensations begin and end with a defining event that changes the economy of man's stewardship responsibilities toward God's revealed will. One might describe man's stewardship responsibilities during the time between Adam and Noah as "walk with God," i.e., live according to God's values and worship him only. Over the centuries between Adam and Noah, mankind walked the wrong way, a way wicked and evil in actions and thoughts, Genesis 6:5. God changed man's responsibilities beginning with Noah. Man's responsibility toward God's will in Noah's time, pre-flood, was to believe God's testimony of coming judgment and get into the ark to be saved from that judgment. Mankind was not ignorant of the change in what they were to believe and do. According to 1 Peter 3:19–20 the Holy Spirit preached that "good news" (of salvation in the ark) through Noah during the time the ark was being built (see my commentary on 1 Peter).

"After the Flood, God gave mankind new stewardship responsibilities through the Noahic covenant, as well as establishing responsibilities (promises to mankind) for himself; see Genesis 8:20–9:17. God's responsibilities in the Noahic covenant continue to the present day. The Noahic covenant is an unconditional covenant as far as God's responsibilities are concerned. God will fulfill his part even if mankind abandons their part. Mankind's stewardship toward his civil responsibilities under the post-flood Noahic covenant continues to the present day. In relation to salvation during the post-flood dispensation, mankind was to live according to God's values and worship him only. This was not a works-based salvation: only by faith in God can one experience the regeneration of soul required to live according to God's values.

"Changes in dispensations are not a hard line at which all the former responsibilities stop and new ones begin. For example, the Noahic Flood defined salvation for a particular generation: believe God's testimony and get into the ark. The post-flood dispensation did not require belief in an imminent judgment by worldwide flood, Genesis 9:11, but did require continued faith in God who gave the covenant. The pre-flood responsibility to walk with and worship the One God who created Adam, brought the flood, and through Noah established a covenant with mankind, did not change. Another example: Israel's responsibilities toward the way of salvation through the ceremonial-sacrificial aspects of the Mosaic Law ended with the responsibility to believe on Jesus the Christ for salvation, but the moral responsibilities required by the law did not change, e.g., Romans 13:8–10. As Calvin said, 'Christians … are called unto holiness. The office of the law is to excite them to the study of purity and holiness, by reminding them of their duty.'[7]

"Beginning with Abraham, God began a new line of stewardship responsibility initially affecting one man, and through him his descendants, and through them the world. Abraham's responsibilities were to walk with God, worship him only, believe in God's promises, and act upon the promises given to him in an unconditional covenant (Genesis 12:1–3; 15; 17; cf. Hebrews 11:8–22). These were the responsibilities of his descendants (through Isaac) for 430 years (Exodus 12:40).

"God changed the economy given to Abraham when he rescued Abraham's descendants from Egypt. As the aftermath reveals, God changed his economy because Israel in Egypt had failed in their

---

[7] Calvin, *Institutes*, 3.19.2.

responsibilities. Many of them had forsaken God for Egyptian idols. They had not returned to the land of the promise but had become citizens of Egypt.

"When God changed the economy from the responsibilities given through Abraham to the responsibilities given through the Mosaic Law, the unconditional promises God made to Abraham were not annulled. What changed was the way in which national ethnic Israel was to worship God: the ceremonial-sacrificial system became the means of approach for salvation and worship. Added was the codification of God's values into precepts to guide the moral and civil aspects of Israeli society. God also gave Israel the responsibility to receive Gentiles into their faith community; for example, Rahab and Ruth.

"The dispensation of the Mosaic Law continued until Jesus Christ was crucified and resurrected, e.g., John 20:22. God initiated a new dispensation and formed the New Testament church, Acts 2, and therein gave both Hebrews and Gentiles a new responsibility: believe on the Lord Jesus Christ to be saved from the penalty due your sin. For the Hebrews/Jews the change in stewardship responsibilities redefined how they would walk with God and worship him only. The Mosaic Law was fulfilled in Christ, Romans 10:4. Saving faith and worship in Christ replaced their approach under the Mosaic Law for salvation and worship.

"The same type of change in responsibilities was also true for the Gentiles. Their stewardship responsibilities had continued unchanged post-flood: walk with God, worship him only, fulfill the terms of the Noahic covenant. But they too had failed. Now the two lines of responsibility—one through Noah, one through Abraham—met in Christ. Peter defined the new stewardship responsibility for the Jews, Acts 2:38, the Samaritans, Acts 2:15, and the Gentiles, Acts 10:47; 15:7–11. Paul explained the change in God's economy toward the Gentiles, e.g., Acts 17:30; Ephesians 2:11–22. The Writer of Hebrews also explained the change in God's economy. Although mankind's civil responsibilities toward the Noahic covenant remain in force, man's responsibility in relation to his salvation is to believe on Jesus as the only Savior, walk with God in Christ, worship him only, proclaim this good news worldwide, and maintain personal preparedness for the imminent return of Christ.

"Mankind's stewardship responsibilities in his relationship toward God have changed throughout history from Adam to Noah to Abraham to Moses to Christ; and will change again in the future. Put another way, from time to time, for reasons that seemed good to God, in response to man's failure to live up to his responsibilities in God's economy, God altered his economy by changing man's responsibilities. God was not surprised by mankind's failures. God's foreordaining choices created a universe that incorporated mankind's failures into his plans and processes to accomplish his purpose."[8]

---

[8] (J. D. Quiggle, Dispensational Eschatology, An Explanation and Defense of the Doctrine 2013)

# Appendix Three

## John Calvin: Journalist, Theologian (1509–1564)

### Background

Born on July 10, 1509, in Noyon, Picardy, France, John Calvin was a law student at the University of Orléans when he first joined the cause of the Reformation. In 1536, he published the landmark text *Institutes of the Christian Religion*, an early attempt to standardize the theories of Protestantism. Calvin's religious teachings emphasized the sovereignty of the scriptures and divine predestination—a doctrine holding that God choses those who will enter Heaven based His omnipotence and grace.

### Leading Figure of Reformation

Calvin lived in Geneva briefly, until anti-Protestant authorities in 1538 forced him to leave. He was invited back again in 1541, and upon his return from Germany, where he had been living, he became an important spiritual and political leader. Calvin used Protestant principles to establish a religious government; and in 1555, he was given absolute supremacy as leader in Geneva.

As Martin Luther's successor as the preeminent Protestant theologian, Calvin was known for an intellectual, unemotional approach to faith that provided Protestantism's theological underpinnings, whereas Luther brought passion and populism to his religious cause.

While instituting many positive policies, Calvin's government also punished "impiety" and dissent against his particularly spare vision of Christianity with execution. In the first five years of his rule in Geneva, 58 people were executed and 76 exiled for their religious beliefs. Calvin allowed no art other than music, and even that could not involve instruments. Under his rule, Geneva became the center of Protestantism, and sent out pastors to the rest of Europe, creating Presbyterianism in Scotland, the Puritan Movement in England and the Reformed Church in the Netherlands.

### Death and Legacy

Calvin died on May 27, 1564, in Geneva, Switzerland. It is unknown where he is buried. Today, Calvin remains widely credited as the most important figure in the second generation of the Protestant Reformation.

*(Biography.com editors 2017)*

# Appendix Four

*The Modern Calendar and Israel's Festivals and Harvests*

"A complete understanding of the Mosaic Tithes requires an understanding of the relationship of modern months to the three mandatory festivals and the crop harvests. The Jewish calendar was based on a lunar cycle of twenty-eight days. The old month ended and a new month began at the first sighting of the sliver of the waxing crescent moon after the new moon.

"Because of the lunar cycle, Jewish months began and ended about half-way through the months on the modern calendar.

"From mid-November—mid-March there were no harvests and no required festivals. However in December there was the Feast of Dedication; a joyous feast with candles and celebrated both in the home and in the Temple.

"The last month of the Jewish year corresponded to the modern mid-February—mid-March."[1]

---

[1] (J. D. Quiggle, Why Christians Should Not Tithe, A History of Tithing and A Biblical Paradigm for Christian Giving 2009)

## Timeline of Jewish Festivals

**Festival** — Passover (Jewish Month of Nisan: 14th. It lasts for 24 hours. No leaven.)

**Festival** — Wave Sheaf of the 1st fruits offering (After Spring Planting BUT Before Spring harvest)

**Festival** — Unleavened Bread (The Jewish Month of Nisan: the 15th to 21st—7 days)

**Festival** — Pentecost (After Wheat and Oat harvest) (Always a Spring Festival. Also known as Shavuot or the Feast of Weeks.)

**Festival** — Trumpets (1st and 2nd Day of the month of Tishri)

**Festival** — Day of Atonement (Yom Kippur—10th Day of the month of Tishri)

**Festival** — Tabernacles (Booths or Tents) Ingather

| SEASON | What's being Harvested |
|---|---|
| Mid March—Mid April | Barley |
| Mid April—Mid May | Wheat, Oats |
| Mid May—Mid June | Pease, Lentils, Vetch |
| Mid June—Mid July | Chickpeas, Grapes |
| Mid July—Mid August | Sesame, Flax, Millet, Grapes |
| Mid August—Mid September | Grapes, Figs, Pomegranates |
| Mid September—Mid October | Grapes, Olives |
| Mid October—Mid November | Olives |
| Mid November—Mid December | Nothing |
| December—Mid March | Nothing. |

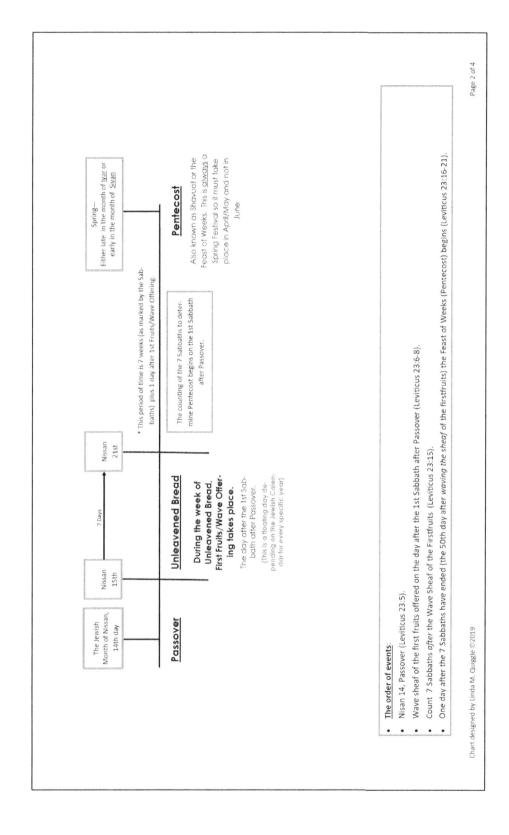

The Jewish Month of Nissan, 14th day

Nissan 15th

7 Days

Nissan 21st

Spring— Either late in the month of *Iyar* or early in the month of *Sivan*

**Passover**

**Unleavened Bread**

**During the week of Unleavened Bread, First Fruits/Wave Offering takes place.**

The day after the 1st Sabbath after Passover.

(This is a floating day depending on the Jewish Calendar for every specific year)

\* This period of time is 7 weeks (as marked by the Sabbaths) plus 1 day after 1st Fruits/Wave Offering.

The counting of the 7 Sabbaths to determine Pentecost begins on the 1st Sabbath after Passover.

**Pentecost**

Also known as Shavuot or the Feast of Weeks. This is *always* a Spring Festival so it must take place in April/May and not in June

**The order of events**:
- Nisan 14, Passover (Leviticus 23:5).
- Wave sheaf of the first fruits offered on the day after the 1st Sabbath after Passover (Leviticus 23:6-8).
- Count 7 Sabbaths *after* the Wave Sheaf of the Firstfruits  (Leviticus 23:15).
- One day after the 7 Sabbaths have ended (the 50th day after *waving the sheaf* of the firstfruits) the Feast of Weeks (Pentecost) begins (Leviticus 23:16-21).

Chart designed by Linda M. Quiggle ©2019

Page 2 of 4

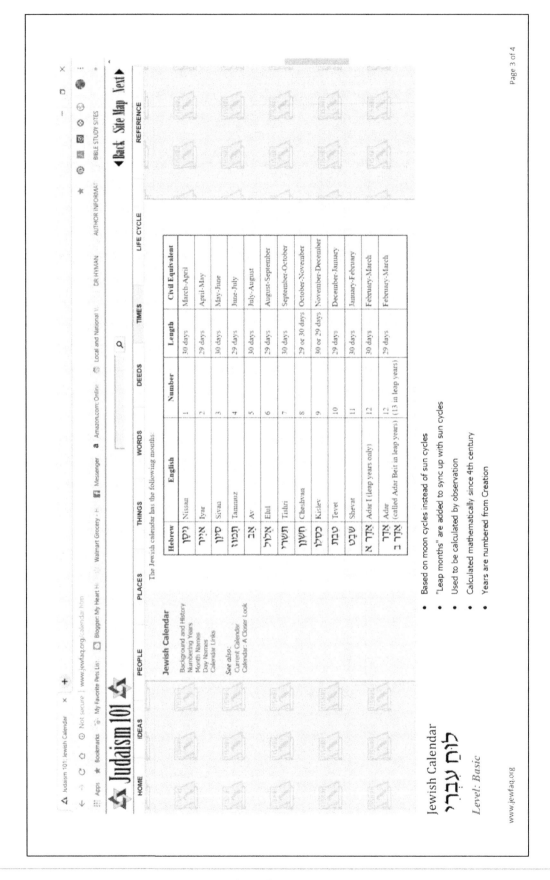

# Jewish Calendar

בלוח עברי

*Level: Basic*

**Jewish Calendar**

Background and History
Numbering Years
Month Names
Day Names
Calendar Links

See also:
Current Calendar
Calendar: A Closer Look

The Jewish calendar has the following months:

| Hebrew | English | Number | Length | Civil Equivalent |
|---|---|---|---|---|
| נִיסָן Nissan | 1 | 30 days | March-April |
| אִיָּר Iyar | 2 | 29 days | April-May |
| סִיוָן Sivan | 3 | 30 days | May-June |
| תַּמּוּז Tammuz | 4 | 29 days | June-July |
| אָב Av | 5 | 30 days | July-August |
| אֱלוּל Elul | 6 | 29 days | August-September |
| תִּשְׁרֵי Tishri | 7 | 30 days | September-October |
| חֶשְׁוָן Cheshvan | 8 | 29 or 30 days | October-November |
| כִּסְלֵו Kislev | 9 | 30 or 29 days | November-December |
| טֵבֵת Tevet | 10 | 29 days | December-January |
| שְׁבָט Shevat | 11 | 30 days | January-February |
| אֲדָר א Adar I (leap years only) | 12 | 30 days | February-March |
| אֲדָר ב Adar (called Adar Beit in leap years) | 12 (13 in leap years) | 29 days | February-March |

- Based on moon cycles instead of sun cycles
- "Leap months" are added to sync up with sun cycles
- Used to be calculated by observation
- Calculated mathematically since 4th century
- Years are numbered from Creation

www.jewfaq.org

BIBLE STUDY SITES

◄ Back  Site Map  Next ►

REFERENCE

## Background and History of the Jewish Calendar

The Jewish calendar is based on three astronomical phenomena: the rotation of the Earth about its axis (a day); the revolution of the moon about the Earth (a month); and the revolution of the Earth about the sun (a year). These three phenomena are independent of each other, so there is no direct correlation between them. On average, the moon revolves around the Earth in about 29½ days. The Earth revolves around the sun in about 365¼ days, that is, about 12.4 lunar months.

The civil calendar used by most of the world has abandoned any correlation between the moon cycles and the month, arbitrarily setting the length of months to 28, 30 or 31 days.

The Jewish calendar, however, coordinates all three of these astronomical phenomena. Months are either 29 or 30 days, corresponding to the 29½-day lunar cycle. Years are either 12 or 13 months, corresponding to the 12.4 month solar cycle.

The lunar month on the Jewish calendar begins when the first sliver of moon becomes visible after the dark of the moon. In ancient times, the new months used to be determined by observation. When people observed the new moon, they would notify the Sanhedrin. When the Sanhedrin heard testimony from two independent, reliable eyewitnesses that the new moon occurred on a certain date, they would declare the rosh chodesh (first of the month) and send out messengers to tell people when the month began.

The problem with strictly lunar calendars is that there are approximately 12.4 lunar months in every solar year, so a 12-month lunar calendar is about 11 days shorter than a solar year and a 13-month lunar is about 19 longer than a solar year. The months drift around the seasons on such a calendar: on a 12-month lunar calendar, the month of Nissan, which is supposed to occur in the Spring, would occur 11 days earlier in the season each year, eventually occurring in the Winter, the Fall, the Summer, and then the Spring again. On a 13-month lunar calendar, the same thing would happen in the other direction, and faster.

To compensate for this drift, the Jewish calendar uses a 12-month lunar calendar with an extra month occasionally added. The month of Nissan occurs 11 days earlier each year for two or three years, and then jumps forward 30 days, balancing out the drift. In ancient times, this month was added by observation: the Sanhedrin observed the conditions of the weather, the crops and the livestock, and if these were not sufficiently advanced to be considered "spring," then the Sanhedrin inserted an additional month into the calendar to make sure that Pesach (Passover) would occur in the spring (it is, after all, referred to in the Torah as Chag he-Aviv, the Festival of Spring!).

A year with 13 months is referred to in Hebrew as Shanah Me'uberet (pronounced shah-NAH meh-oo-BEH-reht), literally: a pregnant year. In English, we commonly call it a leap year. The additional month is known as Adar I, Adar Rishon (first Adar) or Adar Alef (the Hebrew letter Alef being the numeral "1" in Hebrew). The extra month is inserted before the regular month of Adar (known in such years as Adar II, Adar Sheini or Adar Beit). Note that Adar II is the "real" Adar, the one in which Purim is celebrated, the one in which yahrzeits for Adar are observed, the one in which a 13-year-old born in Adar becomes a Bar Mitzvah. Adar I is the "extra" Adar.

In the fourth century, Hillel II established a fixed calendar based on mathematical and astronomical calculations. This calendar, still in use, standardized the length of months and the addition of months over the course of a 19 year cycle, so that the lunar calendar realigns with the solar years. Adar I is added in the 3rd, 6th, 8th, 11th, 14th, 17th and 19th years of the cycle. The current cycle began in Jewish year 5758 (the year that began October 2, 1997). If you are musically inclined, you may find it helpful to remember this pattern of leap years by reference to the major scale: for each whole step there are two regular years and a leap year; for each half-step there is one regular year and a leap year. This is easier to understand when you examine the keyboard illustration below and see how it relates to the leap years above. http://www.jewfaq.org/calendar.htm

# Appendix Five

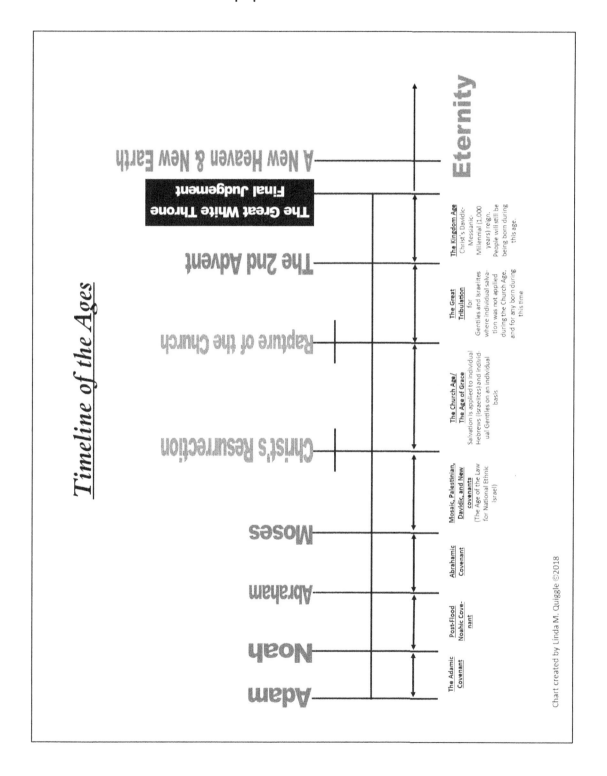

# Appendix Six

## EXORCISM; EXORCIST

ek'-sor-siz'-m, ek'-sor-sist (Exorkistes, from exorkizo, "to adjure" (Mt 26:63)):

### 1. Definition:

One who expels demons by the use of magical formulas. In the strict etymological sense there is no exorcism in the Bible. The term "exorcists" is used once (Acts 19:13) in a way to discredit the professional exorcists familiarly known both among Jews and Gentiles.

### 2. Method of Expelling Demons in the New Testament:

The method of Jesus in dealing with demoniacs was not that of the exorcists. While it is said (Mt 8:16) that He "cast out the spirits with a word," it is abundantly clear that the word in question was not ritualistic but authoritative.

In Lk 4:35 we have a typical sentence uttered by our Lord in the performance of His cures: "Hold thy peace, and come out of him." In Mk 9:29 we have Christ's own emphasis upon the ethical element in dealing with these mysterious maladies: "This kind can come out by nothing, save by prayer." In Mt 12:28 Jesus gives His own explanation of the method and power used in His cures: "But if I by the Spirit of God cast out demons, then is the kingdom of God come upon you."

In Lk 9:1 the terms "authority" and "power" are used in such a way as to show the belief of the evangelists that to cure demon-possession an actual power from God, together with the right to use it, was necessary. This group of passages gives the New Testament philosophy of this dread mystery and its cure. The demons are personal evil powers afflicting human life in their opposition to God. It is beyond man unaided to obtain deliverance from them. It is the function of Christ as the redeemer of mankind to deliver men from this as well as other ills due to sin. Miraculous cures of the same kind as those performed by Christ Himself were accomplished by His disciples in His name (Mk 16:17). The power attributed to "His name" supplies us with the opportunity for a most enlightening comparison and contrast.

### 3. Exorcism in Ethnic and Jewish Writings:

Exorcism among ancient and primitive peoples rests largely upon faith in the power of magical formulas, ordinarily compounded of the names of deities and pronounced in connection with exorcistic rites, upon the bodies of the afflicted. The words themselves are supposed to have power over the demons, and the mere recital of the correct list of names is supposed to be efficacious.

Attention should be called again to the incantation texts of the Babylonians and Assyrians (see, for translations and full exposition of texts, Rogers, Religion of Babylonia and Assyria, 146 ff). In this direction the absurdities and cruelties of superstition have carried men to extreme lengths. In the case of Josephus we are amazed to see how even in the case of an educated man the most abject superstition controls his views of such subjects. In Ant, VIII, v, in speaking of the wisdom of Solomon, he says that "God enabled him to learn that skill which expels demons, which is a science useful and sanitative to him." He also describes, in the same connection, a cure which he alleges to have seen, "in the presence of Vespasian and his sons," performed in accordance with methods of incantation ascribed to Solomon. A ring to which was attached a kind of root mentioned by Solomon was placed at the nostrils of the demoniac and the demon was drawn out through the nostrils. The proof that exorcism had actually taken place was given in the overturning of a basin placed nearby.

The absurdities of this narrative are more than equaled by the story of exorcism told in the Book of Tobit (see Lunge, Apocrypha, 151-53) where the liver and heart of a fish, miraculously caught, are burned upon the ashes of incense, and the resulting smoke drives away a demon. This whole story is well worthy of careful reading for the light it throws upon the unrestrained working of the imagination upon such matters.

In the rabbinical writers the very limit of diseased morbidness is reached in the long and repulsive details, which they give of methods used in exorcism (see Whitehouse, HDB, article "Demon," I, 592b; compare 593b; Edersheim, Life and Times of Jesus the Messiah, II, 775-76).

### 4. Contrasts of New Testament and Popular Methods with Demons:

In most striking contrast with this stand the Biblical narratives. The very point of connection which we have noted is also the point of contrast. The mighty and efficacious word with which Jesus rebuked and controlled demons was no exorcistic formula spoken by rote, but His own living word of holy power. "In the name of Jesus" did not mean that the sacred name formally uttered possessed magical power to effectuate a cure. The ancient Semitic formula, "in the name of," given a deep ethical meaning in the Old Testament, had a still deeper meaning in the New Testament. The proper and helpful use of it meant a reliance upon the presence and living power of Christ from whom alone power to do any mighty work comes (Jn 15:5).

This fundamental difference between the ideas and methods of Jesus and His disciples and current conceptions and usages becomes the more striking when we remember that the lower range of ideas and practices actually prevailed among the people with whom the Lord and His followers were associated. The famous passage (Mt 12:24 and parallel) in which the Pharisees attribute to demoniacal influence the cures wrought by Jesus upon the demonized, usually studied with reference to our Lord's word about the unforgivable sin, is also remarkable for the idea concerning demons which it expresses. The idea which evidently underlies the accusation against Jesus was that the natural way to obtain control over demons is by obtaining, through magic, power over the ruler of demons. In reply to this Jesus maintains that since the demons are evil they can be controlled only by opposition to them in the power of God.

It is most suggestive that we have in Acts 19:13 ff a clear exposition, in connection with exorcism, of just the point here insisted upon. According to this narrative a group of wandering professional Jewish exorcists, witnessing the cures accomplished by Paul, attempted to do the same by the ritualistic use of the name of Jesus. They failed ignominiously because, according to the narrative, they lacked faith in the living Christ by whose power such miracles of healing were wrought, although they were letter-perfect in the use of the formula. This narrative shows clearly what the New Testament understanding of the expression "in my name" implied in the way of faith and obedience.

Here as elsewhere, the chastened mental restraint under which the New Testament was composed, the high spiritual and ethical results of the intimacy of the disciples with Jesus, are clearly manifest.

Our Lord and His disciples dealt with the demoniacs as they dealt with all other sufferers from the malign, enslaving and wasting power of sin, with the tenderness of an illimitable sympathy, and the firmness and effectiveness of those to whom were granted in abundant measure the presence and power of God.

Louis Matthews Sweet **Bibliography Information**
Orr, James, M.A., D.D. General Editor. "Definition for 'EXORCISM; EXORCIST'".
"International Standard Bible Encyclopedia". bible-history.com - ISBE; 1915.

# Appendix Seven

## What was Tyrian dye and why was it important?

Tyrian Dye

-Also referred to as Tyrian purple

-Tyrian Purple was first produced by the Ancient Phoenicians in the city of Tyre

-Tyrian Purple is named after the ancient Phoenician city of Tyre, where it was produced in about 1600 BC.

-Tyrian Purple is produced by a fresh mucous secretion of a small sea snail called murex. The exact species is spiny dye-murex.

-Approximately 60,000 murex animals were required to make one pound of Tyrian Purple.

-From a snail, the murex, the Phoenicians obtained a crimson dye called Tyrian Purple. This was so costly that only kings and wealthy nobles could afford garments dyed with it

-This dye was greatly prized in antiquity because it did not fade, rather it became brighter and more intense with weathering and sunlight. purple was the color of royalty and the designator of status, important because it showed wealth

-The name "Phoenicia" come from the roots meaning "land of purple/red".

-Tyrian dye acted as a source of economy since there is no evidence of other cultures producing dye; so Phoenicians traded the dye.

http://wiki.sjs.org/wiki/index.php/20._What_was_Tyrian_dye_and_why_was_it_important%3F

Accessed 8-8-18

# Appendix Eight

## LINEN: Thread or cloth made of flax

LINEN: lin'-en (badh, "white linen," used chiefly for priestly robes, buts, "byssus," a fine white Egyptian linen, called in the earlier writings shesh; pesheth, "flax," cadhin; bussos, othonion, linon, sindon).

### 1. **History:**

Ancient Egypt was noted for its fine linen (Gen 41:42; Isa 19:9). From it a large export trade was carried on with surrounding nations, including the Hebrews, who early learned the art of spinning from the Egyptians (Ex 35:25) and continued to rely on them for the finest linen (Prov 7:16; Ezek 27:7). The culture of flax in Israel probably antedated the conquest, for in Josh 2:6 we read of the stalks of flax which Rahab had laid in order upon the roof.

Among the Hebrews, as apparently among the Canaanites, the spinning and weaving of linen were carried on by the women (Prov 31:13,19), among whom skill in this work was considered highly praiseworthy (Ex 35:25). One family, the house of Ashbea, attained eminence as workers in linen (1 Ch 4:21; 2 Ch 2:14).

### 2. **General Uses:**

Linen was used, not only in the making of garments of the finer kinds and for priests, but also for shrouds, hangings, and possibly for other purposes in which the most highly prized cloth of antiquity would naturally be desired.

### 3. **Priestly Garments:**

The robes of the Hebrew priests consisted of 4 linen garments, in addition to which the high priest wore garments of other stuffs (Ex 28; 39; Lev 6:10; 16:4; 1 Sam 22:18; Ezek 44:17,18). Egyptian priests are said to have worn linen robes (Herod. ii.37). In religious services by others than priests, white linen was also preferred, as in the case of the infant Samuel (1 Sam 2:18), the Levite singers in the temple (2 Ch 5:12), and even royal personages (2 Sam 6:14; 1 Ch 15:27). Accordingly, it was ascribed to angels (Ezek 9:2,3,11; 10:2,6,7; Dan 10:5; 12:6,7). Fine linen, white and pure, is the raiment assigned to the armies which are in heaven following Him who is called Faithful and True (Rev 19:14). It is deemed a fitting symbol of the righteousness and purity of the saints (Rev 19:8).

## 4. Other Garments:

Garments of distinction were generally made of the same material: e.g. those which Pharaoh gave Joseph (Gen 41:42), and those which Mordecai wore (Est 8:15; compare also Lk 16:19). Even a girdle of fine linen could be used by a prophet as a means of attracting attention to his message (Jer 13:1). It is probable that linen wrappers of a coarser quality were used by men (Jdg 14:12,13) and women (Prov 31:22). The use of linen, however, for ordinary purposes probably suggested unbecoming luxury (Isa 3:23; Ezek 16:10,13; compare also Rev 18:12,16). The poorer classes probably wore wrappers made either of unbleached flax or hemp (Ecclesiasticus 40:4; Mk 14:51). The use of a mixture called sha'aTnez, which is defined (Dt 22:11) as linen and wool together, was forbidden in garments.

## 5. Shrouds:

The Egyptians used linen exclusively in wrapping their mummies (Herod. ii.86). As many as one hundred yards were used in one bandage. Likewise, the Hebrews seem to have preferred this material for winding-sheets for the dead, at least in the days of the New Testament (Mt 27:59; Mk 15:46; Lk 23:53; Jn 19:40; 20:5 ff) and the Talmud (Jerusalem Killayim 9:32b).

## 6. Hangings:
The use of twisted linen (shesh moshzar) for fine hangings dates back to an early period. It was used in the tabernacle (Ex 26:1; 27:9; 35; 36; 38; Josephus, Ant, III, vi, 2), in the temple (2 Ch 3:14),

and no doubt in other places (Mishna, Yoma', iii.4). Linen cords for hangings are mentioned in the description of the palace of Ahasuerus at Shushan (Est 1:6).

## 7. Other Uses:

Other uses are suggested, such as for sails, in the imaginary ship to which Tyre is compared (Ezek 27:7), but judging from the extravagance of the other materials in the ship, it is doubtful whether we may infer that such valuable material as linen was ever actually used for this purpose. It is more likely, however, that it was used for coverings or tapestry (Prov 7:16), and possibly in other instances where an even, durable material was needed, as in making measuring lines (Ezek 40:3).

Ella Davis Isaacs
**Bibliography Information**
Orr, James, M.A., D.D. General Editor.
"Definition for 'linen'".
"International Standard Bible Encyclopedia". bible-history.com - ISBE; 1915.

# Appendix Nine

## SKIN DISEASES: Boils

It is likely that the word "boil" as used in the Bible covered many types of skin diseases, such as pustules, simple boils, carbuncles, abscesses and infected glands.

Boils, as we know them today, are usually caused by staphylococci. These germs are normally present on the surface of the skin, and do no harm unless there is some kind of injury to the skin, allowing the germs to get inside and proliferate. The body reacts with its defense of leucocytes, and in the battle that ensues germs, leucocytes and debris may form a painful pocket of pus that we call a boil. If the boil is single and comes to a head, it ruptures and recovery follows.

A carbuncle is much like a collection of boils in a limited area. The infection runs deeper than an ordinary boil and has several openings. It is commonly located in the back of the neck. It usually covers an area several inches in diameter, and sometimes is fatal.

An abscess may be minor, but frequently is deep, involving important structures of the body, such as muscles, lungs, brain, liver, spleen, kidney, bowel and appendix.

Hezekiah's boil must have been a carbuncle or deep abscess, as his life hung in the balance when he was afflicted with it. Job's boils were superficial, or they would have resulted in his death. The boils of the sixth Egyptian plague probrobably were extremely painful superficial boils.

The Babylonians used boils in its broader sense. Recently archeologists dug up a Babylonian tablet which stated that if a physician cut into a boil and the patient died, the physician would have both his hands cut off. If the patient happened to be a slave, the physician's hands were spared, but he had to buy another slave for the owner of the patient. So, the doctor had to be extremely careful when he lanced an abscess or a boil.

https://www.biblicaltraining.org/library/diseases-bible

# Appendix Ten

## Tax Collectors in the Roman Empire

The Tax Collector or Tax Gatherer is the Greek word "*telones*" and the King James Version of the Bible translates the word "publican." He was contracted by Rome to collect taxes for the government during New Testament times. The Greek word *telones* were really NOT the publicans. Publicans were wealthy men, usually non-Jewish, who contracted with the Roman government to be responsible for the taxes of a particular district of the imperial Roman state. These publicans would often be backed by military force.

The *telones* tax collectors to which the New Testament refers (with the exception of Zacchaeus?) were employed by publicans to do the actual collecting of taxes within the areas where they lived. These men were Jews, usually not very wealthy, who could be seen in the Temple (Luke 18:13). They were probably very familiar with the people from whom they collected taxes.

The Publican collected income tax for Rome. Sometime around 200 B.C. the Roman Senate found it fitting to farm the *vectigalia* (direct taxes) and the *portoria* (customs) to capitalists, who agreed to pay a substantial sum into the *publicum* (treasury) and so received the name of publicani.

The Roman class who handled the contracts and financial arrangements were called *equites*. They often went further in their dealings with the publicani and formed a joint-stock *societas* (company) partnership with them or one of their agents *magister* (manager). This manager usually resided at Rome and conducted business and paying profits to all partners through the *submagistri* (officer) who lived among the provinces. Directly under their authority were the *portitores* (customhouse officers) who would examine all goods, whether imported or exported, assess the value, wrote out a ticket and enforced payment. They would live within the province where they were stationed and come into contact with all classes of the population. It was these *portitores* who were referred to as the Tax Gatherers (*telones*) in the New Testament.

These tax-gatherers were usually Jews and would collect taxes for Rome and it was understood that they were to keep a "fraction" for themselves. There was really no real way to prevent that fraction from assuming great proportions, and in fact fraudulent exactions were encouraged. Although there were some honorable exceptions, the publicans, great and small, were really extortioners.

Luke 3:12-15 "Then tax collectors also came to be baptized, and said to him, "Teacher, what shall we do?" And he said to them, "Collect no more than what is appointed for you." Likewise the soldiers asked him, saying, "And what shall we do?" So he said to them, "Do not intimidate anyone or accuse falsely, and be content with your wages."

The Jewish people were outraged by the Publicans and regarded them as traitors and apostates. They were considered defiled by their constant contact with the heathen, even Rome's willing instruments of oppression. Zacchaeus was called a "chief tax-gatherer" (Greek: 'architelones') in Luke 19:2 and his kind were utterly despised. Yet Jesus showed mercy on him: *Luke 19:8-10 "Then Zacchaeus stood and said to the Lord, "Look, Lord, I give half of my goods to the poor; and if I have taken anything from anyone by false accusation, I restore fourfold." And Jesus said to him, "Today salvation has come to this house, because he also is a son of Abraham; for the Son of Man has come to seek and to save that which was lost."*

In Augustus's day (27 B.C.-A.D. 14) the practice of selling tax-collection contracts to joint-stock companies ceased, and tax collectors were put on the public payroll. Thus a kind of Internal Revenue Service was established and continued through the rest of the NT period.

### Edersheim makes an interesting comment:

"The Talmud distinguishes two classes of publicans-the tax-gatherer in general (Gabbai) and the Mokhes or Mokhsa, who was specially the douanier, or customhouse official. Although both classes fell under the rabbinic ban, the douanier-such as Matthew was-was the object of chief execration. And this because his exactions were more vexatious and gave more scope to rapacity. The Gabbai, or tax-gatherer, collected the regular dues, which consisted of ground, income, and poll tax. . . . If this offered many opportunities for vexatious exactions and rapacious injustice, the Mokhes might inflict much greater hardship upon the poor people. There was a tax and duty upon all imports and exports; on all that was bought and sold; bridge money, road money, harbor dues, town dues, etc. The classical reader knows the ingenuity which could invent a tax and find a name for every kind of exaction, such as on axles, wheels, pack animals, pedestrians, roads, highways; on admission to markets; on carriers, bridges, ships, and quays; on crossing rivers, on dams, on licenses-in short, on such a variety of objects that even the research of modern scholars has not been able to identify all the names. But even this was as nothing compared to the vexation of being constantly stopped on the journey, having to unload all one's pack animals, when every bale and package was opened, and the contents tumbled about, private letters opened, and the Mokhes ruled supreme in his insolence and rapacity" (Edersheim, Life and Times of Jesus the Messiah, 1:515 ff.).

These tax collectors gathered several different types of taxes. Rome levied upon the Jews a land tax, a poll tax, even a tax for the operation of the Temple. There were different kinds of taxes for every territory. For example, since some provinces, like Galilee, were not under an imperial governor, taxes remained in the province rather than going to the imperial treasury at Rome. This is one reason why the Pharisees in Judea (an imperial province) came to ask Jesus, "Is it lawful to pay taxes to Caesar, or not?" (Matt 22:17).

Levi or Matthew, gathered the customs on exports and imports and taxes (Matt 9:9-11; Mark 2:14, etc.). The office for "receipt of custom" was at city gates, on public roads, or bridges. Levi's post was on the great road between Damascus and the seaports of Phoenicia.

Zacchaeus' headquarters were in Jericho, which was a great center for the balsam trade. In fact this was the territory where the famed Marc Anthony purchased balsam plantations for Queen Cleopatra. It is interesting that when Jesus was in Jericho He preferred to eat at the publican's house than any of the priests who lived in Jericho, who were said to have numbered over 10,000, which reveals the honor that He bestowed upon Zacchaeus and the scorn for the Jewish priesthood.

*https://www.bible-history.com/taxcollectors/TAXCOLLECTORSHistory.htm*

# Appendix Eleven

## Widows in Jewish Tradition

By Rabbi Louis Jacobs

"There are numerous injunctions in the Bible to care for widows and orphans and to avoid taking advantage of their situation of having no husband or father to protect them.

Protecting Rights

The underprivileged to whom the poor man's tithe was to be given include 'the orphan, and the widow'. (Deuteronomy 26:12). The warning not to oppress a widow or an orphan is stated with full rigor: 'You shall not ill-treat any widow or orphan. If you do mistreat them, I will heed their cry as soon as they cry out to Me, and My anger shall blaze forth and I will put you to the sword, and your own wives shall become widows and your children orphans (Exodus 22:21-24)'.

The Midrash stresses the word 'any' in the verse to include 'the widow of a king' and in the Jewish tradition generally concern for the feelings of the widow and orphan applies even to wealthy widows and orphans, not only to the poor and disadvantaged.

From Talmud ic times onwards the courts appointed a guardian for orphans, a trustworthy man who would administer faithfully and voluntarily the estate they had inherited from their father. The prophet Isiah urges his people: 'Uphold the rights of the orphan; defend the cause of the widow (Isaiah 1:17)'.

Job, protesting his innocence, says: 'For I saved the poor man who cried out, the orphan who had none to help him. I received the blessing of the lost, I gladdened the heart of the widow' (Job 29:12-13).'

In Jewish law as developed by the Rabbis, while orphans inherit their father's estate, a widow does not inherit her husband's estate. But, the *ketuhah* consists of a settlement on the estate from which the widow is entitled to maintain until she remarries... While a few pious men in the past did refuse to marry a widow, the normal attitude throughout the ages is permissive and there are many instances of pious scholars marrying widows."

(Jacobs Reprinted from The Jewish Religion: A Companion, published by Oxford University Press.)

# Appendix Twelve

## Pharisees

Pronounced [FARE uh sees], and known as 'separated ones.'

There were a religious and political party in Palestine in New Testament times. The Pharisees were known for insisting that the law of God be observed as the scribes interpreted it and for their special commitment to keeping the laws of tithing and ritual purity.

The Pharisees had their roots in the group of faithful Jews known as the Hasidim (or Chasidim). The Hasidim arose in the second century B.C. when the influence of Hellenism on the Jews was particularly strong and many Jews lived little differently than their Gentile neighbors. But the Hasidim insisted on strict observance of Jewish ritual laws.

When the Syrian King Antiochus IV tried to do away with the Jewish religion, the Hasidim took part in the revolt of the Maccabees against him. Apparently from the movement of faithful Hasidim came both the Essenes—who later broke off from the other Jews and formed their own communities—and the Pharisees, who remained an active part of Jewish life. Indeed, during the period of independence that followed the revolt, some of the Greek rulers who controlled Palestine favored the Pharisaic party.

As a result of the favoritism, Pharisees came to be represented on the Sanhedrin, which was the supreme court and legislative body of the Jews. At times, the Pharisees even dominated the assembly. In New Testament times, Pharisaic scribes, though probably in the minority, were still an effective part of the Sanhedrin.

The Pharisees also believed it was important to observe all the laws of God. But they were especially known for their commitment to keep the laws of tithing and ritual purity. These were the laws that other people were less careful about observing. Since Pharisees found that other Jews were not careful enough about keeping the laws of tithing and ritual purity, they felt it was necessary to place limits on their contacts with other Jews as well as the Gentiles. For example, they could not eat in the home of a non-Pharisee, since they could not be sure that the food had been properly tithed and kept ritually pure.

Pharisees observed the Law carefully as far as appearances went, but their hearts were far from God. Their motives were wrong because they wanted the praise of men (Matthew 6:2,5,16; 23:5–7). They also had evil desires that were hidden by their pious show (Matthew 23:35–28). That is why Pharisees are often called hypocrites: their hearts did not match their outward appearance.

*For more information concerning Pharisees refer to: Nelson's Illustrated Bible Dictionary; https://en.wikipedia.org/wiki/Pharisees; https://www.biblestudytools.com/dictionary/pharisees.*

# Appendix Thirteen

## Tax Collectors in the Roman Empire

"The Tax Collector or Tax Gatherer is the Greek word "*telones*" and the King James Version of the Bible translates the word "publican." He was contracted by Rome to collect taxes for the government during New Testament times. The Greek word *telones* were really NOT the publicans. Publicans were wealthy men, usually non-Jewish, who contracted with the Roman government to be responsible for the taxes of a particular district of the imperial Roman state. These publicans would often be backed by military force.

"The *telones* tax collectors to which the New Testament refers (with the exception of Zacchaeus?) were employed by publicans to do the actual collecting of taxes within the areas where they lived. These men were Jews, usually not very wealthy, who could be seen in the Temple (Luke 18:13). They were probably very familiar with the people from whom they collected taxes.

"The Publican collected income tax for Rome. Sometime around 200 B.C. the Roman Senate found it fitting to farm the *vectigalia* (direct taxes) and the *portoria* (customs) to capitalists, who agreed to pay a substantial sum into the *publicum* (treasury) and so received the name of publicani.

"The Roman class who handled the contracts and financial arrangements were called *equites*. They often went further in their dealings with the publicani and formed a joint-stock *societas* (company) partnership with them or one of their agents *magister* (manager). This manager usually resided at Rome and conducted business and paying profits to all partners through the *submagistri* (officer) who lived among the provinces. Directly under their authority were the *portitores* (customhouse officers) who would examine all goods, whether imported or exported, assess the value, wrote out a ticket and enforced payment. They would live within the province where they were stationed and come into contact with all classes of the population. It was these *portitores* who were referred to as the Tax Gatherers (*telones*) in the New Testament.

"These tax-gatherers were usually Jews and would collect taxes for Rome and it was understood that they were to keep a "fraction" for themselves. There was really no real way to prevent that fraction from assuming great proportions, and in fact fraudulent exactions were encouraged. Although there were some honorable exceptions, the publicans, great and small, were really extortioners.

*"Luke 3:12-15 "Then tax collectors also came to be baptized, and said to him, "Teacher, what shall we do?" And he said to them, "Collect no more than what is appointed for you." Likewise the soldiers asked him, saying, "And what shall we do?" So he said to them, "Do not intimidate anyone or accuse falsely, and be content with your wages.""*

"The Jewish people were outraged by the Publicans and regarded them as traitors and apostates. They were considered defiled by their constant contact with the heathen, even Rome's willing instruments of oppression. Zacchaeus was called a "chief tax-gatherer" (Greek: 'architelones') in Luke 19:2 and his kind were utterly despised. Yet Jesus showed mercy on him: *Luke 19:8-10 "Then Zacchaeus stood and said to the Lord, "Look, Lord, I give half of my goods to the poor; and if I have taken anything from anyone by false accusation, I restore fourfold." And Jesus said to him, 'Today salvation has come to this house, because he also is a son of Abraham; for the Son of Man has come to seek and to save that which was lost."*

"In Augustus's day (27 B.C.-A.D. 14) the practice of selling tax-collection contracts to joint-stock companies ceased, and tax collectors were put on the public payroll. Thus a kind of Internal Revenue Service was established and continued through the rest of the NT period.

### "Edersheim makes an interesting comment:

"The Talmud distinguishes two classes of publicans-the tax-gatherer in general (Gabbai) and the Mokhes or Mokhsa, who was specially the douanier, or customhouse official. Although both classes fell under the rabbinic ban, the douanier-such as Matthew was-was the object of chief execration. And this because his exactions were more vexatious and gave more scope to rapacity. The Gabbai, or tax-gatherer, collected the regular dues, which consisted of ground, income, and poll tax. . . . If this offered many opportunities for vexatious exactions and rapacious injustice, the Mokhes might inflict much greater hardship upon the poor people. There was a tax and duty upon all imports and exports; on all that was bought and sold; bridge money, road money, harbor dues, town dues, etc. The classical reader knows the ingenuity which could invent a tax and find a name for every kind of exaction, such as on axles, wheels, pack animals, pedestrians, roads, highways; on admission to markets; on carriers, bridges, ships, and quays; on crossing rivers, on dams, on licenses-in short, on such a variety of objects that even the research of modern scholars has not been able to identify all the names. But even this was as nothing compared to the vexation of being constantly stopped on the journey, having to unload all one's pack animals, when every bale and package was opened, and the contents tumbled about, private letters opened, and the Mokhes ruled supreme in his insolence and rapacity" (Edersheim, Life and Times of Jesus the Messiah, 1:515 ff.).

"These tax collectors gathered several different types of taxes. Rome levied upon the Jews a land tax, a poll tax, even a tax for the operation of the Temple. There were different kinds of taxes for every territory. For example, since some provinces, like Galilee, were not under an imperial governor, taxes remained in the province rather than going to the imperial treasury at Rome. This is one reason why the Pharisees in Judea (an imperial province) came to ask Jesus, "Is it lawful to pay taxes to Caesar, or not?" (Matt 22:17).

"Levi or Matthew, gathered the customs on exports and imports and taxes (Matt 9:9-11; Mark 2:14, etc.). The office for "receipt of custom" was at city gates, on public roads, or bridges. Levi's post was on the great road between Damascus and the seaports of Phoenicia.

"Zacchaeus' headquarters were in Jericho, which was a great center for the balsam trade. In fact this was the territory where the famed Marc Anthony purchased balsam plantations for Queen Cleopatra. It is interesting that when Jesus was in Jericho He preferred to eat at the publican's house than any of the priests who lived in Jericho, who were said to have numbered over 10,000, which reveals the honor that He bestowed upon Zacchaeus and the scorn for the Jewish priesthood. "

*https://www.bible-history.com/taxcollectors/TAXCOLLECTORSHistory.htm*

# Appendix Fourteen

## BEG; BEGGAR; BEGGING

### 1. No Law Concerning Beggars or Begging in Israel:

It is significant that the Mosaic law contains no enactment concerning beggars, or begging, though it makes ample provision for the relief and care of "the poor in the land." Biblical Hebrew seems to have no term for professional begging, the nearest approach to it being the expressions "to ask (or seek) bread" and "to wander." This omission certainly is not accidental; it comports with the very nature of the Mosaic law, the spirit of which is breathed in this, among other kindred provisions, that a poor Hebrew who even sold himself for debt to his wealthy brother was allowed to serve him only until the Jubilee (See JUBILEE), and his master was forbidden to treat him as a sl ave (Lev 25:39). These laws, as far as actually practiced, have always virtually done away with beggars and begging among the Jews.

### 2. Begging Not Unknown to the Ancient Jews:

Begging, however, came to be known to the Jews in the course of time with the development of the larger cities, either as occurring among themselves, or among neighboring or intermingling peoples, as may be inferred from Ps 59:15; compare 109:10, where Yahweh is besought that the children of the wicked may be cursed with beggary, in contra-distinction to the children of the righteous, who have never had to ask bread (Ps 37:25, "I have been young, and now am old; yet have I not seen the righteous forsaken, nor his seed asking (English Versions, "begging") bread." For the Hebrew expression corresponding to "begging" see Ps 59:15, "They shall wander up and down for food"; and compare Ps 119:10, "Let me not wander," etc.

### 3. Begging and Alms-taking Denounced in Jewish Literature:

The first clear denunciation of beggary and almstaking in Jewish literature is found in Ecclesiasticus (Sirach) 40:28-30, where the Hebrew for "begging" is to "wander," ete, as in Ps 59:15, according to the edition of Cowley and Neubauer; Oxford, 1897. There as well as in Tobit, and in the New Testament, where beggars are specifically mentioned, the word eleemosune has assumed the special sense of alms given to the begging poor (compare Tobit 4:7,16,17; 12:8-11; Ecclesiasticus (Sirach) 3:14,30; 7:10; 16:14; Mt 6:2-4; 20:30-34; Mk 10:46-52; Lk 11:41; 12:33; Jn 9:1-41; Acts 9:36; 10:2,4,31; 24:17).

### 4. Professional Beggars a Despised Class:

As to professional beggars, originally, certainly, and for a long time, they were a despised class among the Hebrews; and the Jewish communities are forbidden to support them from the general charity fund (BB, 9a; Yoreh De`ah, 250, 3). But the spirit of the law is evinced again in that it is likewise forbidden to drive a beggar away without an alms (ha-Yadh ha-Chazaqah, in the place cited 7 7).

### 5. In the Gospel Age:

Begging was well known and beggars formed a considerable class in the gospel age. Proof of this is found in the references to almsgiving in the Sermon on the Mount (Mt 5 through 7 and parallels), and in the accounts of beggars in connection with public places, e.g. the entrance to Jericho. (Mt 20:30 and parallels), which was a gateway to pilgrims going up to Jerusalem to the great festivals and in the neighborhood of rich men's houses (Lk 16:20), and especially the gates of the Temple at Jerusalem (Acts 3:2). This prevalence of begging was due largely to the want of any adequate system of ministering relief, to the lack of any true medical science and the resulting ignorance of remedies for common diseases like ophthalmia, for instance, and to the impoverishment of the land under the excessive taxation of the Roman government (Hausrath, History of New Testament Times, I, 188 (Eng. translation Williams and Norgate), compare Edersheim, Life and Times of Jesus, II, 178). That begging was looked down upon is incidentally evidenced by the remark of the unjust steward, "To beg I am ashamed" (Lk 16:3); and that, when associated with indolence, it was strongly condemned by public opinion appears from Sirach (40:28-30).

The words used for "beg," "beggar" of English Versions of the Bible in the New Testament differ radically in idea: in those formed from aiteo (Mk 10:46; Lk 16:3; 18:35; Jn 9:8 the Revised Version (British and American)) the root idea is that of "asking," while ptochos (Lk 16:20,22) suggests the cringing or crouching of a beggar. But see Mt 5:3 where the word for "humble" is ptochos.

### 6. A Change in Modern Times:

A marked change has come over Jewish life in modern times, in this as well as in other respect. Since the 17th century the Jewish poor in many parts of the world have made it a practice, especially on Fridays and on the eves of certain festivals, to go systematically from house to house asking alms. In parts of Europe today it is a full-grown abuse: crowds of Jewish beggars push their way and ply their trade about the synagogue doors (Abrahams, EB, article "Alms," 310). So the Jewish beggar, in spite of the spirit of the law and ancient Jewish custom, has, under modern conditions too well known to require explanation here, become a troublesome figure and problem in modern Jewish society. For such beggars and begging, see Jew Encyclopedia, articles "Schnorrers," "Alms," etc., and for another kind of begging among modern Jews, and collections for poverty-stricken Jewish settlers in Israel, see the articles "Chalukah," "Charity," etc.

LITERATURE.

Saalschiutz, Arch. der Hebraer, II, chapter xviii (Konigsberg, 1855-56);

Riehm Handworterbuch zu den Buchern des A T, under the word "Almosen "; compare Jew Encyclopedia, HDB, and Encyclopedia B, arts, "Alms"; and Abrahams,

Jewish Life in the Middle Ages, chapters xvii, xviii (Philadelphia, 1896);

Mackie, Bible Manners and Customs; Day, The Social Life of the Hebrews.

George B. Eager
**Bibliography Information**
Orr, James, M.A., D.D. General Editor.
"Definition for 'BEG; BEGGAR; BEGGING'".
"International Standard Bible Encyclopedia".
bible-history.com - ISBE; 1915.

# Appendix Fifteen

Excerpt from, "A Private Commentary on The Bible: Matthew's Gospel;" © 2016 James D. Quiggle; Pages 203–206

## The Unpardonable Sin

"First, if you are a believer who is concerned you may have committed this sin, then you haven't. A person who commits this sin against the Holy Spirit feels no need for repentance. One of the distinguishing marks of a Christian is that he or she knows sin is wrong. Whenever a Christian commits a sin, he or she feels remorse and godly sorrow, and comes to the Lord in repentance and confession, to be forgiven and restored to fellowship with God. A believer has accepted by faith everything this sin denies: Christ as Savior and the work of the Holy Spirit in his or her life. A believer will not commit this sin: the Holy Spirit will not let him.

"If you are an unbeliever worried about this sin, then the fact that you worried, seeking to understand sin, the Savior, and salvation, indicates you have not committed this sin. People who have committed the unpardonable sin don't worry about it. They have made up their mind to reject the salvation God offers them in Jesus Christ. You would not be here if you had committed this sin.

"What is the unpardonable sin? First, let's read the Scripture.

> Matthew 12:31–32 Because of this I say to you, every sin and blasphemy will be forgiven men, but blasphemy against the Spirit will not be forgiven. 32 And whoever speaks a word against the son of man, it will be forgiven him; but whoever may speak against the Holy Spirit, it will not be forgiven him, neither in this age nor in the one coming.

> Mark 3:29 But whoever may blasphemes against the Holy Spirit never has forgiveness to the eternity, but is guilty of eternal sin.

> Luke 12:10 And every person who will say a saying against the son of man, it will be forgiven him; but the person having blasphemed against the Holy Spirit will not be forgiven.

"If we look at the context of Matthew, Mark, and Luke, and the larger context of the Holy Spirit's operations in the gospels, we can find several defining characteristics that will help us understand this sin.

> The Scribes and Pharisees kept on accusing Jesus of casting out demons by the power of Satan. They did not make this accusation once; the Greek verb tense is, "they kept on saying." They were hardened in their opposition to Jesus, and made an accusation deliberately intended to

slander him and the Holy Spirit, in order to turn people away from faith in Jesus. Their slander was a habitual act that indicated an underlying unrepentant attitude of unbelief and opposition toward God.

The Scribes and Pharisees knew, from Scripture, that the power by which Jesus performed these miracles was in fact the power of the Holy Spirit.

The Old Testament Scriptures said the messiah would come in the power of the Spirit of the Lord to heal people, Isaiah 11:12, 49:8.

John the Baptist had told Israel that messiah was immediately coming and would baptize with the Holy Spirit.

Jesus quoted Isaiah 61:1, 2 as validating his ministry, therefore the authority and power by which he cast out demons was the Holy Spirit.

"The Pharisees understood that they were slandering the Holy Spirit. To blaspheme is to slander or defame. They recognized that the Holy Spirit was the source of the power by which Jesus performed miracles, but they said that the source of Jesus' power to cast out demons was demonic, satanic. This slander, said Jesus, cannot be forgiven.

"Can this sin occur today?

The people who originally committed this sin were religious people who knew the Scriptures, saw Christ and the Spirit working in the world, and made a decision to slander the Holy Spirit and reject Christ as their messiah. They were unbelievers.

However, this sin is not simply disbelief or rejection of Jesus as Savior. That sin of unbelief is always forgivable, up to the moment of death. Remember, Jesus said, "every sin and blasphemy will be forgiven men," except slander against the Holy Spirit. The unpardonable sin is slander against the Holy Spirit. Slander is not accidental, it is knowing and deliberate.

"It is possible to commit this sin today under two circumstances.

One way is to agree with the Scribes and Pharisees that the work of the Holy Spirit is really the work of Satan. Satan is actively at work in the religions of the world, even where the name "Christian" is over the door. But, Satan cannot be the power behind Christian worship, fellowship, obedience, and serving God. Satan does not produce morality, ministry, unity, and fellowship according to the scriptures. Satan does not forgive sin and change people's lives from sinner to saved. To see these particular things at work in the lives of sinners being saved and believers living like Christ, and then to reject it as evil or demonic or satanic, is to agree with the Scribes and Pharisees that the power of the Holy Spirit is the power of Satan. It is appropriate to recognize Satan at work, even when he is doing a bad imitation of God; it is inappropriate to recognize the Holy Spirit at work and knowingly slander him.

The second way to commit this sin is to reject the Spirit by rejecting his work to save sinners. I am not speaking of the temporary rejection—often more than one time—that can be part of the process used by the Spirit to convict a sinner and bring him/her to faith and salvation. I am speaking of rejection throughout all of life into physical death. The power of physical death is to seal the soul into its spiritual state at the time of death. A lifetime of rejecting the Spirit's work to convict and save results in a soul never convicted and never saved.

The Holy Spirit is the divine Person who applies the truth of God to the sinner's soul. The Holy Spirit is the One who applies the grace of God that brings salvation. Any unbeliever truly seeking to understand sin, the Savior, and salvation will in some measure participate in the external benefits the Holy Spirit brings to his people: the morality, ministry, unity, and fellowship of Christianity. But if, after experiencing the external benefits of work of the Spirit, the unbeliever then rejects the Spirit's testimony, and permanently (throughout his/her lifetime) turns away from faith in Christ, the unrepentant attitude toward the things of God is a sin against the Spirit. This person is not repentant, and without repentance there is no forgiveness.

"Finally, why can't this sin be forgiven? It is less a matter of God forgiving, than the sinner repenting. Remember, the unbelieving Jews unrepentantly rejected Christ and the Spirit's witness. Their unrepentant attitude is seen in their slander of the Spirit. This same attitude is seen in the book of Acts, where time and again they rejected the works of the Spirit as being God's works. The works of the Spirit make this statement to every sinner: 'Here is Jesus the Savior who will save you from your sins.' That testimony requires a choice. A person either repents of his sin, or he rejects the Spirit's witness. To reject Jesus out of ignorance is forgivable. To reject the Holy Spirit is to be knowingly unrepentant; if one does not repent, then he or she cannot be forgiven.

Anyone who is truly repentant, no matter how shameful or serious his or her sin might be, can be saved. But, the person who rejects the Spirit's witness of their sin, and their need for repentance and forgiveness, that person's sin is unpardonable, because he or she refuses to walk the path that leads to salvation.

# Appendix Sixteen

## Viperous Snakes

"All viperids have a pair of relatively long hollow fangs that are used to inject <u>venom</u> from glands located towards the rear of the upper jaws, just behind the eyes. Each of the two fangs is at the front of the mouth on a short <u>maxillary</u> bone that can rotate back and forth. When not in use, the fangs fold back against the roof of the mouth and are enclosed in a membranous sheath. This rotating mechanism allows for very long fangs to be contained in a relatively small mouth.

The left and right fangs can be rotated together or independently. During a strike, the mouth can open nearly 180° and the <u>maxilla</u> rotates forward, erecting the fangs as late as possible so that the fangs do not become damaged, as they are brittle. The jaws close upon impact and the muscular sheaths encapsulating the venom glands contract, injecting the venom as the fangs penetrate the target. This action is very fast; in defensive strikes, it will be more a stab than a bite. Viperids use this mechanism primarily for immobilization and digestion of prey. Pre-digestion occurs as the venom contains proteases which degrade tissues. Secondarily, it is used for self-defense, though in cases with non-prey, such as humans, they may give a <u>dry bite</u> (not inject any venom). A dry bite allows the snake to conserve their precious reserve of venom, because once it has been depleted, it takes time to replenish, leaving the snake vulnerable. In addition to being able to deliver dry bites, vipers can inject larger quantities of venom into larger prey targets, and smaller amounts into small prey. This causes the ideal amount of pre-digestion for the lowest amount of venom.

"Almost all vipers have <u>keeled scales</u>, a stocky build with a short tail, and due to the location of the venom glands, a triangle-shaped head distinct from the neck. The great majority have vertically elliptical, or slit-shaped, <u>pupils</u> that can open wide to cover most of the eye or close almost completely, which helps them to see in a wide range of light levels. Typically, vipers are nocturnal and ambush their prey.

"Compared to many other snakes, vipers often appear rather sluggish. Most are <u>ovoviviparous</u>, holding eggs inside their bodies, where they hatch inside and emerge living. However, a few lay eggs in nests. Typically, the number of young in a clutch remains constant, but as the weight of the mother increases, larger eggs are produced, yielding larger young.

## Venom

"Viperid venoms typically contain an abundance of protein-degrading enzymes, called proteases, that produce symptoms such as pain, strong local swelling and necrosis, blood loss from cardiovascular damage complicated by coagulopathy, and disruption of the blood-clotting system. Death is usually caused by collapse in blood pressure. This is in contrast to elapid venoms that generally contain neurotoxins that disable muscle contraction and cause paralysis. Death from elapid bites usually results from asphyxiation because the diaphragm can no longer contract. However, this rule does not always apply; some elapid bites include proteolytic symptoms typical of viperid bites, while some viperid bites produce neurotoxic symptoms.

"Proteolytic venom is also dual-purpose: firstly, it is used for defense and to immobilize prey, as with neurotoxic venoms; secondly, many of the venom's enzymes have a digestive function, breaking down molecules in prey

"Items, such as lipids, nucleic acids, and proteins. This is an important adaptation, as many vipers have inefficient digestive systems.

"Due to the nature of proteolytic venom, a viperid bite is often a very painful experience and should always be taken seriously, though it may not necessarily prove fatal. Even with prompt and proper treatment, a bite can still result in a permanent scar, and in the worst cases, the affected limb may even have to be amputated. A victim's fate is impossible to predict, as this depends on many factors, including the species and size of the snake involved, how much venom was injected (if any), and the size and condition of the patient before being bitten. Viper bite victims may also be allergic to the venom and/or the antivenom.

## Behavior

"These snakes can decide how much venom to inject depending on the circumstances. The most important determinant of venom expenditure is generally the size of the snake; larger specimens can deliver much more venom. The species is also important, since some are likely to inject more venom than others, may have more venom available, strike more accurately, or deliver a number of bites in a short time. In predatory bites, factors that influence the amount of venom injected include the size of the prey, the species of prey, and whether the prey item is held or released. The need to label prey for chemosensory relocation after a bite and release may also play a role. In defensive bites, the amount of venom injected may be determined by the size or species of the predator (or antagonist), as well as the assessed level of threat, although larger assailants and higher threat levels may not necessarily lead to larger amounts of venom being injected.

*https://en.wikipedia.org/wiki/Viperidae*

# Appendix Seventeen

**"Question:** When is the Rapture going to occur in relation to the Tribulation?

**"Answer**: The timing of the rapture in relation to the tribulation is one of the most controversial issues in the church today. The three primary views are pre-tribulation (the rapture occurs before the tribulation), mid-tribulation (the rapture occurs at or near the mid-point of the tribulation), and post-tribulation (the rapture occurs at the end of the tribulation). A fourth view, commonly known as pre-wrath, is a slight modification of the mid-tribulational position.

"First, it is important to recognize the purpose of the tribulation. According to Daniel 9:27, there is a seventieth 'seven' (seven years) that is still yet to come. Daniel's entire prophecy of the seventy sevens (Daniel 9:20-27) is speaking of the nation of Israel. It is a time period in which God focuses His attention especially on Israel. While this does not necessarily indicate that the church could not also be present, it does bring into question why the church would need to be on the earth during that time.

"The primary Scripture passage on the rapture is 1 Thessalonians 4:13-18. It states that all living believers, along with all believers who have died, will meet the Lord Jesus in the air and will be with Him forever. The rapture is God's removing His people from the earth. A few verses later, in 1 Thessalonians 5:9, Paul says, 'For God did not appoint us to suffer wrath but to receive salvation through our Lord Jesus Christ.' The book of Revelation, which deals primarily with the time period of the tribulation, is a prophetic message of how God will pour out His wrath upon the earth during the tribulation. It seems inconsistent for God to promise believers that they will not suffer wrath and then leave them on the earth to suffer through the wrath of the tribulation. The fact that God promises to deliver Christians from wrath shortly after promising to remove His people from the earth seems to link those two events together.

"Another crucial passage on the timing of the rapture is Revelation 3:10, in which Christ promises to deliver believers from the 'hour of trial' that is going to come upon the earth. This could mean two things. Either Christ will protect believers in the midst of the trials, or He will deliver believers out of the trials. Both are valid meanings of the Greek word translated 'from.' However, it is important to recognize what believers are promised to be kept from. It is not just the trial, but the 'hour' of trial. Christ is promising to keep believers from the very time period that contains the trials, namely the tribulation. The purpose of the tribulation, the purpose of the rapture, the meaning of 1 Thessalonians 5:9, and the interpretation of Revelation 3:10 all give clear support to the pre-tribulational position. If the Bible is interpreted literally and consistently, the pre-tribulational position is the most biblically-based interpretation."

# Appendix Eighteen

## FOUR KINGDOMS IN SCRIPTURE

The concept of the Davidic-Messianic Kingdom was once considered too prominent in Scripture to deny. As Edersheim said,

> A Kingdom of God without a King; a Theocracy without the rule of God; a perpetual Davidic Kingdom without a "Son of David"—these are antinomies (to borrow the term of Kant) of which neither the Old Testament, the Apocrypha, the Pseudepigraphic writings, nor Rabbinism were guilty.[1]

Unfortunately, in the modern world, men have taught themselves to deny the kingdom. A literal Davidic Kingdom where the Son of David—Jesus the Christ—rules on the earth is denied by many theologies of the modern age. Therefore it will be necessary to discuss the kingdom in general terms before describing the Davidic-Messianic-Millennial Kingdom.

A kingdom consists of ruler, ruled, domain, and duration. For example, the statue in Daniel 2 teaches these aspects of a kingdom, Daniel 2:37–39. Scripture teaches four aspects of kingdom in relation to God and his Christ.[2]

*The Universal Kingdom*. God's universal rule over his creation. The ruler is the Triune God; the ruled are all created beings; the domain is the universe; the duration is eternity.

*The Mystery Kingdom*. The ruler is Christ; the ruled are saved and unsaved during the New Testament church dispensation; the domain is the earth; the duration is the New Testament church dispensation.

*The Spiritual Kingdom*. The ruler is Christ; the ruled are the saved of the New Testament church dispensation; the domains are the spirit and material domains; the duration is the New Testament church dispensation.

*The Davidic-Messianic-Millennial Kingdom*. The kingdom promised in the Davidic covenant, 2 Samuel 7:11b–17; 1 Chronicles 17:10b–15. The ruler is Christ; the ruled are physically living mankind; the domain is the earth; the duration is one thousand years. The raptured and resurrected New Testament church will reign with Christ in this kingdom, 2 Timothy 2:12; Revelation 5:10, as will the resurrected Tribulation saints, 20:4–6.

*The Universal, Mystery, and Spiritual kingdoms are present today*. The Mystery and Spiritual Kingdoms do not describe a spiritualized form of the Davidic-Messianic Kingdom, but describe

---

[1] Edersheim, *Life and Times*, 1:265, n. 3.
[2] Some propose a fifth kingdom, the Theocratic Kingdom, which was God's rule over Israel from Moses to Zedekiah (the last king of Jerusalem).

Christ's rule during the New Testament church dispensation. The character of the Mystery and Spiritual Kingdoms is described below.

*The Mystery Kingdom*. During the New Testament church dispensation there are persons who outwardly join themselves to the community of believers with a false profession of saving faith. Some believe they are saved. Others join for the moral and material benefits of associating with a loving, kind, righteous, and generous people. Still others are schismatics, heretics, or apostates who want to appear as Christ-believers while teaching and practicing their own false doctrines.

To outward appearances these persons are saved. This is the visible church—the church the world sees—apparently composed of saved persons, but in reality composed of saved and unsaved. The visible church is the Mystery Kingdom in which Christ seems to rule all who profess salvation in his name. The Mystery Kingdom is most clearly seen in the irregularities of Christian practice and the inconsistencies of doctrine, testimony, and witness among the churches. It is a mystery because a false profession of faith cannot always be discerned by outward appearances; because saved and unsaved alike appear to be members of Christ's kingdom. One might think the mystery will be resolved at the rapture, but professors of faith will continue as though nothing has happened. The mystery will be resolved when Christ returns and inaugurates his Davidic Kingdom, because only the saved will enter into the Davidic-Messianic-Millennial Kingdom.

*The Spiritual Kingdom* is the faith-community of all the saved from Pentecost to the rapture. The members of the Spiritual Kingdom look toward the realization and completed form of the Davidic Kingdom when Christ returns at his second advent. The members of the Spiritual Kingdom (the New Testament church) will participate with Christ in the Davidic Kingdom, Romans 8:17; Revelation 1:6; 5:10, and enter into the Eternal dispensation, Revelation 21, 22.

## KINGDOM OF GOD, KINGDOM OF HEAVEN

The New Testament identifies the four kingdoms described above through the terms "kingdom of God" and "kingdom of heaven." The phrase "kingdom of God" occurs seventy times in the New Testament. It occurs fifty-five times total in Matthew (5 times), Mark (15), Luke (33), and John (2); it occurs fifteen times total in Acts (7), Romans (1) Corinthians (4), Galatians (1), Colossians (1), 2 Thessalonians (1).

Jesus used "kingdom of God" and "kingdom of heaven" interchangeably, so they share some characteristics, but they are not the same kingdom. The Acts and epistles use "kingdom of God" as synonymous with the Mystery Kingdom, the Spiritual Kingdom, and the Davidic-Messianic-Millennial Kingdom. Context establishes meaning, see Acts 1:3; 8:12; 14:22; 18:8; 20:25; 28:23, 31; Romans 14:17; 1 Corinthians 4:20; 6:9, 10; 15:50; Galatians 5:21; Colossians 4:11; 2 Thessalonians 1:5.

Context also establishes meaning for the phrase "kingdom of heaven," which occurs only in Matthew's Gospel, a total of thirty-two times. The announcement "the kingdom of heaven is at hand," 3:2; 4:17; 10:7 proclaimed the Davidic-Messianic Kingdom prophesied by the prophets. In 5:3, 10, 19, 20, the phrase referred to the Davidic-Messianic Kingdom, as does 7:21; 8:11; 11:12. The phrase referred to the Mystery Kingdom in Matthew 13:11, 24, 31, 33, 44, 45, 47, 52; 18:23; 20:1; 22:2; 25:1, 14. The phrase referred to the Spiritual Kingdom in Matthew 16:19; 18:1, 3, 4; 19:14, 23; 23:13.

There are, then, four kingdoms in Scripture. There are three which exist now: the Universal, Mystery, and Spiritual. There is one yet-future, the Davidic-Messianic-Millennial Kingdom, which is the subject of this chapter.

## THE DAVIDIC-MESSIANIC KINGDOM OFFERED AND REJECTED

When John Baptist and Jesus Christ began to preach their message (Matthew 3:2; 4:17), they proclaimed "the kingdom of heaven is at hand." When Jesus sent out the twelve, Matthew 10:7, he told them to preach "the kingdom of heaven is at hand" to "the lost sheep of the house of Israel," but do not preach this message to Gentiles or Samaritans. In Matthew 9:35 Jesus "went all about the cities and villages . . . preaching the good news of the kingdom." In Mark 1:14–15 Jesus preached the good news of the "kingdom of God," that it was "at hand" (a synonymous use of kingdom of God for kingdom of heaven). Jesus said he was sent to preach the kingdom of God, Luke 4:43, as were the twelve sent by him, Luke 9:2 (both synonymous uses of kingdom of God for kingdom of heaven).

There is no doubt that in these and similar verses the message was understood by those hearing it as declaring that the Messianic kingdom promised to King David was about to be fulfilled. Whether or not the Israelis believed the message is a separate issue to be discussed below. The point here is that Jesus offered national ethnic Israel the Messianic Kingdom.

*Excerpt from, Dispensational Eschatology, An Explanation and Defense of the Doctrine*

©2013 James D. Quiggle; Pages 205-208

# References

n.d. *10 Yard Trees Gone Bad.* Accessed February 21, 2019. https://www.thoughtco.com/yard-trees-gone-bad-1343518.

Alexander, J.A. 1864, Reprint 1980. *Commentary on the Gospel of Mark.* Klock & Clock Christian Publishers.

n.d. *Ancient Tax Collectors.* Accessed January 18, 2019. https://www.bible-history.com.

Arnot, William. 1865. *Parables of Our Lord.* London, U.K.: Reprint of the 1865 edition by T. Nelson.

Barnes, Albert. Reprinted from the 1884-1885 edition by Blackie & Son, London. *Notes on the New Testament.* Baker Book House.

Beasley-Murray, George R. 1999. *Word Biblical Commentary, Volume 36 (second edition), John.* N/A: Thomas Nelson, Inc.

2018. *Bible Gateway.* Accessed 2018.

2018. *Bible Hub.* Accessed 2018.

n.d. *Biblical Training: Diseases of the Bible.* Accessed 8 9, 2018. https://www.biblicaltraining.org/library/diseases-bible.

Biography.com editors. 2017. *John Calvin Biography.* April 27. Accessed November 16, 2018. https://www.biography.com/people/john-calvin-9235788.

Bock, Darrell L. 1996. *Luke - Volume 2: 9:51-24:53—Baker Exegetical Commentary on the New Testament.* Grand Rapids, Michigan: Baker Academic a Division of Baker Publishing Group.

Brooks, James A. 1991. *The New American Commentary: Mark.* Vol. Volume 23. Broadman Press.

Calvin, John. Originally printed 1610 in London, England. *Commentary on a Harmony of the Evangelists.* Reprinted in 1996 in Grand Rapids, MI: Baker Book House.

—. 1996. *Commentary on a Harmony of the Evangelists, Matthew, Mark, and Luke.* Translated by William Pringle. Vol. One. Twenty-Two vols. Grand Rapids,MI: Baker Books.

Cole, Canon R.A. Reprinted, 1999; copyright 1989. *The Gospel According to Mark, an Introduction and Commentary (Tyndale New Testament Commentaries).* Leicester, England/Grand Rapids, MI: Inter-Varsity Press/William B. Eerdmans Publishing Company.

Cox, Steven L. and Easley, Kendell H. [2007]. *HCSB Harmony of the Gospels.* Nashville, TN: Holman Bible Publishers.

Daniel, Orville E. 1996. *A Harmony of the Four Gospels: The New International Version, Second Edition.* Grand Rapids, MI: Baker Academic a division of Baker Publishing Group.

n.d. *Darnel.* Accessed 10 1, 2018. https://en.wikipedia.org/wiki/Lolium_temulentum.

Dickson, David. 1981. *A Brief Exposition of the Evangel of Jesus Christ According to MATTHEW.* Carlisle, PA: The Banner of Truth/Kingsport Press, Inc.

2018. *Dictionary.* Accessed 2018.

Edwards, James R. 2002. *The Gospel according to Mark.* Grand Rapids, Michigan/Cambridge, UK: William B. Eerdmans Publishing Company/Apollos.

English, E Schuyler. 1943. *Studies in the Gospel According to Mark.* New York, NY: Our Hope (Aro C Gaebelein, Inc.).

Evans, Craig A. 2001. *Mark 8:27 - 16:20.* Vol. Volume 34b. Thomas Nelson Publishers.

France, R.T. 1985. *The Gospel According to Matthew, an Introduction and Commentary (Tyndal New Testament Commentaries).* Leicester, England/Grand Rapids, Michigan: Inter-Varsity Press/William B. Eerdmans Publishing Company.

Freeman, James M. Reprinted 1972. *Manners and Customs of the Bible.* Logos International.

—. Reprinted 1972 from the original of Nelson and Phillips New York. *Manners and Customs of the Bible.* Logos International.

Geldenhuys, Norval. 1951. *Commentary on The Gospel of Luke (The English text with Introduction exposition and notes).* Grand Rapids, Michigan: William B. Eerdmans Publishing Company.

2018. *Got Questions.* Accessed 2018.

Guelich, Robert A. 1989. *Mark 1 - 8:26; Word Biblical Commentary.* Vol. 34a. Dallas: Wofd Books.

Hagner, Donald A. 1993. *Matthew 1 - 13; Word Biblical Commentary.* Vol. 33a. Dallas: Word Books.

—. 1995. *Matthew 14 - 28; Word Biblical Commentary.* Vol. 33b. Dallas: Word Books.

Hudson, Bob. 1978 CCCM Music. "Humble Thyself in the Sight of the Lord." Brentwood-Benson Music Publishing, Inc.

Hutchinson, George. 1657, 1841 edition. *The Gospel of John.* Edinburgh, Scotland: Banner of Truth Trust 1972, 1985.

1915. *International Standard Bible Encyclopedia (ISBE) .* Accessed 08 09, 2018. https://www.bible-history.com/isbe/B/BEG;+BEGGAR;+BEGGING/.

J. Julius Scott, Jr. Copyright 1996. *Pharisees.* Edited by Walter A. Elwell. Baker Book House Company. Accessed 08 16, 2018. https://www.biblestudytools.com/dictionary/pharisees/.

Jacobs, Rabbi Louis. Reprinted from The Jewish Religion: A Companion, published by Oxford University Press. *Widows in Jewish Tradition.* Accessed 08 03, 2018. https://www.myjewishlearning.com/article/widows-in-jewish-tradition/.

Jones, J.D. 1992 (Originally in 1914). *Commentary on Mark (Originally: The Gospel according to St. Mark)*. Grand Rapids, MI 49501 (Originally London, UK): Kregel Publications, a division of Kregal, Inc. (Originally by Religious Tract Society).

Keller, Phillip. 1970, 1978, 1982, 1996. *The Shepherd Trilogy: A Shepherd Looks at the 23rd Psalm*. Grand Rapids, MI 49530: Zondervan.

—. 1996. *The Shepherd Triology: A Sheperd Looks at the Good Shepherd*. Grand Rapids, MI 79530: Zondervan.

—. 1970, 1978, 1982, 1996. *The Shepherd Triology: A Shepherd Looks at the Lamb of God*. Grand Rapids, MI 49530: Zondervan.

Kimber, Brandon. 2018. *American Gospel: Christ Alone*. DVD. Directed by Brandon Kimber. Produced by Transition Studios. American Gospel Motion Picture, LLC. Accessed March 05, 2019.

Kostenberger, Andreas J. 2004. *John; Baker Exegetical Commentary on the New Testament*. Grand Rapids, MI: Baker Academic; a division of Baker Publishing Group.

Lockyer, Sr., Herbert; General Editor. 1986. *Nelson's Illustrated Bible Dictionary*. Nashville: Thomas Nelson, Inc.

Maclaren, Alexander. Reprinted 1977. *Expositions of Holy Scripture - St. Matthew - Chaps. IX to IVII*. Grand Rapids, MI: Baker Book House.

Morgan, G. Campbell. 1943. *The Parables and Metaphors of Our Lord*. Old Tappan, NJ: Fleming H. Revell Company.

Morris, Leon. Reprinted 1999. *Luke, an Introduction and Commentary (Tyndale New Testament Commentaries)*. Grand Rapids, MI: William B. Eerdmans Publishing Company.

—. [1992]. *The Gospel according to Matthew (The Pillar New Testament Commentary)*. Grand Rapids, MI: William B. Eerdmans Publishing Co.

n.d. *Mustard Plant*. Accessed 10 7, 2018. https://en.wikipedia.org/wiki/Mustard_plant.

Nolland, John. 1986. *Luke 1 - 9:20, Word Biblical Commentary*. Vol. 35a. Dallas: Word Books.

—. 1993. *Luke 18:35 - 24:53; Word Biblical Commentary*. Vol. 35c. Dallas: Word Books.

—. 1993. *Luke 9:21-18:34; Word Biblical Commentary*. Vol. Volume 35b. Dallas: Word Books.

Orr, James M.A., D.D. n.d. *Beg, Beggar, Begging*. Accessed January 23, 2019. https://www.bible-history.com.

Orr, James M.A., D.D. n.d. *https://www.bible-history.com/isbe/l/linen*. Accessed January 23, 2019. https://www.bible-history.com.

Publishers, Tyndale House. 2015. *The One Year Chronological Bible, New Living Translation*. Carol

Stream, IL: Tyndale House Publishers.

—. [2015]. *The One Year Chronological Bible, New Living Translation*. Carole Stream IL: Tyndale House Publishers, Inc;.

Quiggle, James D. 2014. *A Private Commentary on the Bible: John 1–12*. Createspace.

—. 2014. *A Private Commentary On the Bible: John 1-12*. Create Space by James D. Quiggle.

—. 2017. *A Private Commentary on the Bible: Matthew's Gospel*. Create Space.

—. 2011. *ADAM AND EVE, A Biography and Theology*. Print: Createspace.

—. 2017. *Angelology, A True History of Angels*. CreateSpace.

—. 2017. *Christian Living and Doctrine*. CreateSpace a Division of Amazon.

—. 2018. "Dictionary of Doctrinal Words: Explanatory and Practical Definitions Of Select Biblical, Theological, and Doctrinal Terms." *Dictionary of Doctrinal Words*. 2018: Create Space, 08.

—. n.d. *Dispensational Escatology*. Create Space.

—. 2013. *Dispensational Eschatology, An Explanation and Defense of the Doctrine*. CreateSpace.

—. 2019. "Hermeneutics: Blasphemy Against the Holy Spirit." *Facebook; private group: Calvinist Dispensational Baptists*. Edited by Matt Sherro. January. Accessed January 2019.

—. 2019. "Hermeneutics: The Lost Sheep, the Lost Coin, the Lost Son." Canyon, TX: James D. Quiggle, February 1.

—. 2009. *Why Christians Should Not Tithe, A History of Tithing and A Biblical Paradigm for Christian Giving*. Eugene, OR: Wipf and Stock.

Quiggle, Linda Marie. 2018. *God Revealed by His Attributes*. CreateSpace.

Rich, Tracey R. n.d. *Judaism 101 - The Jewish Calendar*. Accessed December 28, 2018. http://www.jewfaq.org/calendar.htm.

Ryrie, Charles Caldwell. 1995. *Ryrie Study Bible, Expanded Edition*. Chicago, Illinois: The Moody Bible Institute of Chicago.

2011. *Salt Evaporation Pond*. August. Accessed 08 03, 2018. https://en.wikipedia.org/wiki/Salt_evaporation_pond.

Stewart, Roy A. 1975. *Judicial Procedures in New Testament Times*. February. Accessed 08 13, 2018. https://biblicalstudies.org.uk/pdf/eq/1975-2_094.pdf.

Strong, James. n.d. *The Exhaustive Concordance of the Bible*. McLean, VA: Macdonald Publishing Co.

Thomas Nelson Publishers. 1986. *Nelson's Illustrated Bible Dictionary*. Nashville, TN: Thomas Nelson Publishers.

Questions.org, Got, ed. n.d. "What Does It Mean to Bind the Strong Man."
*https://www.gotquestions.org.* Accessed February 29, 2019.
https://www.gotquestions.org/bind-the-strongman.html.

Wight, Fred H. Reprinted 1980 from Original by The Moody Bible Institute of Chicago, 1953. *Manners and Customs of Bible Lands.* Chicago: Moody Press.

Wuest, Kenneth S. Reprinted in a Three-volume edition 1973 (Originally published separately in 1950). *Wuest's Word Studies from the Greek New Testament (for the English Reader): Mark In the Greek New Testament.* Vols. One: Mark - Romans - Galatians - Ephesians and Colossians. Three vols. Grand Rapids, MI: Wm. B. Eerdmans Publishing Company.

Zodhiates, Spiros. 1993. *The Complete Word Study Dictionary New Testament.* Chattanooga: AMG Publishers.

Zodhiates, Sprios. 1993. *The Complete Word STudy Dictionary New Testament.* Chattanooga: AMG Publishers.

Made in the USA
Monee, IL
22 April 2021

66410403R00116